Football's Mis-Direction Wing-T

With Multi-Points of Attack

Carl O. "Bill" Gentry

COACHES CHOICE™

ISBN: 978-1-60679-003-8
Library of Congress Control Number: 2008920156
Cover design & book layout: Roger W. Rybkowski
Diagrams: Antonio J. Perez and Roger W. Rybkowski
Front cover photo: Bill Wood
Back cover photo: Jack Newsom

Coaches Choice
P.O. Box 1828
Monterey, CA 93942
www.coacheschoice.com

Dedication

To my family…
My wife, Mary;
My children—Billy and his wife, Anita;
Marcy and her husband, Allen Baysinger;
Tom and his wife, Kris.
To my grandchildren—Travis, Haley, Adam
Clayton, Samuel, and Zachary.

Acknowledgments

The 38 teams of players whose super effort and dedication to the game of football made all the success happen...I salute you.

The 38 coaching staffs who taught the skills and motivated those teams to reach their highest potential...I salute you.

Thanks to the parents and the fans for your support. There is nothing like a "packed house," where people are "hanging from the rafters," to motivate a super-performance from the young men on the field...*I salute you.*

Contents

Preface

In 1996, I retired after 38 consecutive years of head football coaching. During those 38 years, the teams I had the opportunity and honor of coaching won 305 football games—an average of slightly more than eight wins per season. This book is a tribute to all of those players, coaches, and their families who provided the effort and dedication to "make it happen."

The primary purpose of this second edition of this book—as it was with the first edition—is to share ideas, insights, and information about an offense that we used during my last 22 years as a head coach that played a major role in our success. This revised edition features a new chapter that covers the split-end side attack. This attack was used to supplement our basic offense for a number of reasons, not the least of which was the fact that it caused defenses to adjust to new offensive looks (alignments).

Truth be known, after 22 years of running the same type of offense, I literally collected a "mountain" of material. This book details only the major aspects of the misdirection wing-T offense with three points of attack. If the book helps coaches in any way with their football program, then the time and energy to write it will have been well worth the effort.

B.G.

PART I:
UNDERSTANDING THE BASICS

©Elsburgh Clarke Photography

1

The Concept

In 1974, after 16 years of running three different offenses, I decided to adapt the wing-T of the 1950s and 60s to a more up-to-date view that suited our way of thinking. As a direct result of that decision, our "three points of attack" philosophy off of the wing-T mis-direction series was developed. Logically, we named this offensive scheme, "Mis-Direction Wing-T With Multi-Points of Attack." The fundamental concept of this scheme is to produce three possible points of attack on each snap of the football in a true mis-direction style of offense. The basic intent of this offense is to control defensive pursuit and cause hesitation of the linebackers. In order to more clearly demonstrate the three points of attack concept, this chapter details several basic sets and their descriptive points, which are diagrammed and discussed.

©Mark Faram

The Counter Break

❑ *Left Formation:*

• 18" splits in the line and off the ball maximum.

❑ *Right Formation:*

• 18" splits in the line and off the ball maximum.

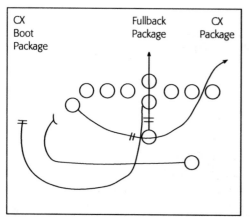

Diagram 1-1

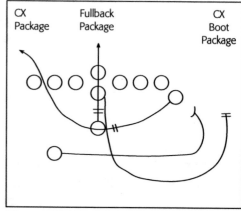

Diagram 1-2

Fullback—assumes a three-point stance, with his helmet six feet from the quarterback's butt. He dives every snap and does not bend his course to avoid the quarterback.

Halfback—assumes a two-point stance behind the tackle, with his toes two-feet deeper than the fullback's heels. He gets a wall position on the defensive end for the counter-boot play.

The Wing—assumes a two-point stance, with his toes in 1/8 of a turn. He takes a position with a 12" split from the outside foot of the tight end. He runs a half-moon course and comes to the quarterback for the ball or a fake.

The Quarterback—pivots out of the fullback's path and either fakes or gives the ball to him (as called in the huddle). Next, the quarterback runs a half-moon course and either gives or fakes the ball to the counter back and continues his counter-boot course. The counter boot is always "run-first" intent.

Coaching Point

> On the counter break, the fullback should assume a three-point stance, with his helmet six feet from the quarterback's butt. He dives every snap and should not bend his course to avoid the quarterback.

Right-Fly Call:
- Same plays as the left call

Left-Fly Call:
- Same plays as the right call

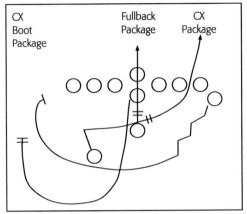

Diagram 1-3

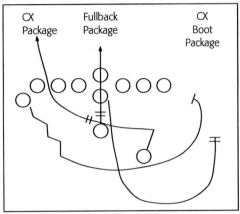

Diagram 1-4

Left-Double Call:
- Same plays as the left formation and the right-fly formation
- Three formations to the left

Right-Double Call:
- Same plays as the right formation and the left-fly formation
- Three formations to the right

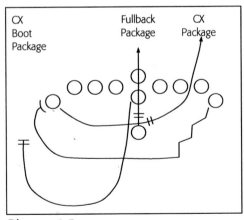

Diagram 1-5

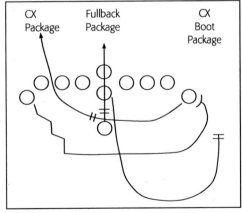

Diagram 1-6

All plays are mirrored. The backs are not flip-flopped. The snap count is in cadence in order to coordinate the one-count, full-speed fly. The fly man must be at his halfback position at the snap.

The Sweep Break

❑ *Left-Formation Call:*

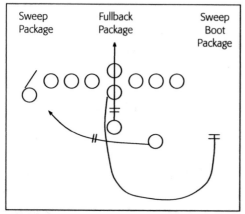

Diagram 1-7

❑ *Right-Formation Call:*

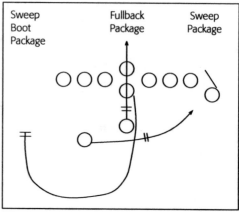

Diagram 1-8

As in the counter break, the fullback dives and either gets the ball or a fake. The halfback runs his sweep break and gets the ball or a fake. The wing blocks on sweeps and is a receiver on the boots. The quarterback initially either gives or fakes to the fullback. He then gives or fakes to the halfback, and finally continues his half-moon course to run his boot or fake it.

❑ *Right-Fly Formation Call:*
  • Same plays as the left call

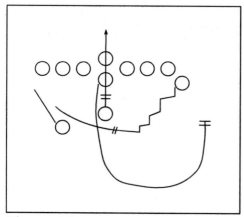

Diagram 1-9

❑ *Left-Fly Formation Call:*
  • Same plays as the right call

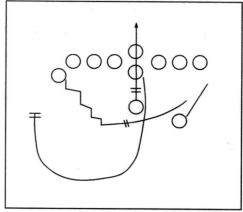

Diagram 1-10

❏ *Left-Double Call:*
  • Same plays as the left call and the right-fly call
  • Three sweep formations to the left

❏ *Right-Double Call:*
  • Same plays as the right call and the left-fly call
  • Three sweep formations to the *right*

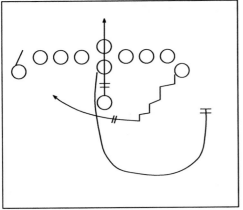

Diagram 1-11

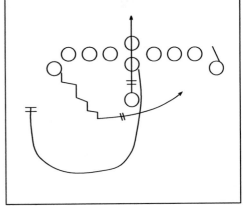

Diagram 1-12

2

Method of Operation

Holes and Labeling of Plays

A standardized system is employed for identifying the holes and labeling the plays. This system helps clarify where each player must go on a play and what his responsibilities are on that particular play. Diagram 2-1 illustrates how the holes are designated—even numbers to the right and odd numbers to the left.

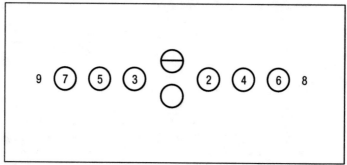

Diagram 2-1

- The formation is called first, e.g., right, left fly, and right double. Right double means that the left wing will fly, which puts the offense in a right formation at the snap of the ball. The flip side of these formations are left, right fly, and left double.
- The first digit signals the series break.
- The second digit refers to the hole to be attacked.
- A word added means that the play involves special action or a blocking change.
- The system for calling plays allows the players to clearly understand what each play entails. For example, the play "right 28 sweep" involves the following: right formation; 20 series; the hole is 8 sweep.

The Snap-Count Method

The count system is in cadence, so that the one-count fly series can be coordinated.

"READY"—We never snap on ready.
"SET"—First count
"HIT"—Second count
"HIT"—Third count
"HIT"—Fourth count

The first-sound snaps are mixed by using the word, "GO." A "READY" call is not made if the offense is going on first sound. The ball is not snapped on "GO" if it is a fly play. The offense can also make a live call before the "READY" call.

Series Calls (First Digit)

❑ *20 Series:*
  • The fullback will dive (Diagram 2-2).

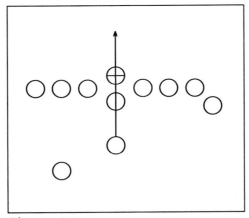

Diagram 2-2

Coaching Point

The count system is in cadence, so that the one-count fly series can be coordinated.

□ *30 Series:*
- On counters, the fullback plugs away from the hole (Diagram 2-3).
- On sweeps, the fullback kicks out or escorts the ball.
- The playside guard does not pull (Diagram 2-4).

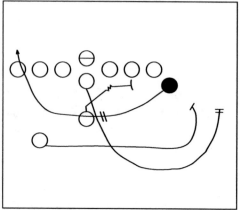

Diagram 2-3

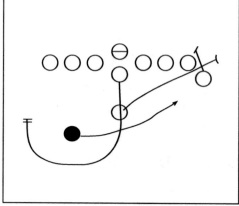

Diagram 2-4

□ *40 Series:*
- The fullback carries the ball on special plays.
- The blocking scheme remains the same as for the 20 series.
- 40 series sweep (Diagram 2-5).
- The slant-option (Diagram 2-6).

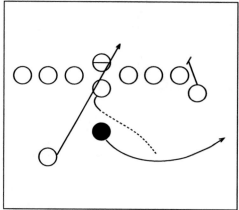

Diagram 2-5

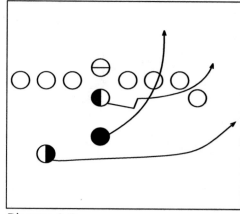

Diagram 2-6

- The wham (Diagram 2-7):

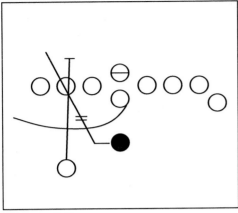

Diagram 2-7

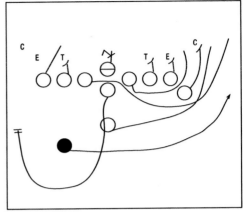

Diagram 2-8

- ❏ *50 Series:*
  - The same as the 30 Series for the fullback and the same as the 20 Series for the offensive line.
  - Hence, 20 and 30 equals 50.
  - Diagram 2-8 illustrates an example of a 50 Series play—the Right 58 Base Sweep.

Teaching the Backs

Executing proper courses is vital to this offense. Smooth connections on the "fake and take" must be made without hesitation or change in courses, in order to produce a "quick take-off" on each and every snap. At first, no ball is used when the backfield breaks are being taught. It is explained to everyone that they are getting the ball. Once an acceptable level of production is achieved, a ball is then used. Initially, the backs are divided into two groups—a quarterback and fullback group and a halfback and wing group to work on the fundamental moves. Next, the whole backfield is brought back together to initially practice the backfield breaks at learning speed and then to progress to full speed. The spacing strap is used to get the required land marks.

> **Coaching Point**
>
> *The ability of the backs to execute proper courses is vital to this offense.*

Coaching Point —————————————————————————————

> When teaching backs, the whole backfield is brought back together to initially practice the backfield breaks at learning speed and then to progress to full speed.

❏ *The Counter Break and Progression (Diagrams 2-9, 2-10, and 2-11)*
- Right call (Diagram 2-9):
- Left-fly call (Diagram 2-10):

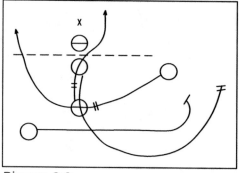

Diagram 2-9

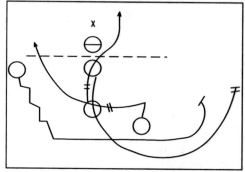

Diagram 2-10

- Right-double call (Diagram 2-11):

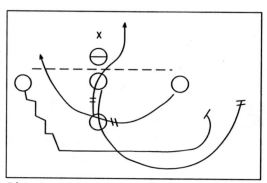

Diagram 2-11

- Repeat the progression from left formations.

Coaching Point —————————————————————————————

> The team should now be able to run the fullback trap, the counter, and the counter boot from all six formations.

❏ *The Sweep Break (Diagrams 2-12, 2-13, and 2-14):*
  • Right call (Diagram 2-12):   • Left-fly call (Diagram 2-13)

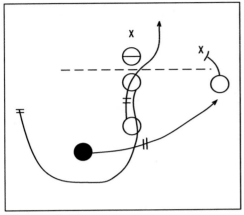

Diagram 2-12   Diagram 2-13

        •   Right-double call (Diagram 2-14):

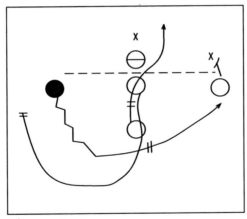

Diagram 2-14

  • Repeat to the left.

Coaching Point

The team should now be relatively proficient at running the wide fullback trap, the sweeps, and the sweep boot from all six formations.

Fundamental Techniques for Each Backfield Position on the Counter Break

❑ *The Counter Break from the Right Call—Repeat to Left (Diagrams 2-15 to 2-18)*
   • The fullback (Diagram 2-15):

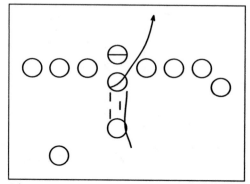

Diagram 2-15

The fullback steps first with his foot opposite the hole. He then receives the ball or the fake on his second step. He plants and cuts on his third step. He covers the ball or the fake with both forearms until he clears the linebackers. He sells the carry on fakes and tries to get tackled.

   • The wingback (Diagram 2-16):

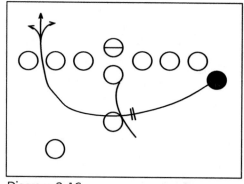

Diagram 2-16

The wing points his inside toe on a half-moon path. He then takes a course through the fullback's shoulder pads, comes to the quarterback, and continues his course to cut upfield between the tackle and the tight end, with his shoulders parallel to the line of scrimmage, as he enters the hole. If he is carrying the ball, he runs to daylight. If he is faking, he makes some cuts and sells the counter.

• The halfback (Diagram 2-17):

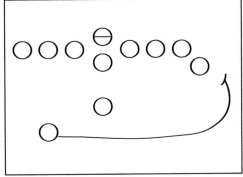

Diagram 2-17

The halfback sprints flat out, with full speed, to beat the quarterback and get an "outside-in" blocking position on the first, unblocked opponent.

• The quarterback (Diagram 2-18):

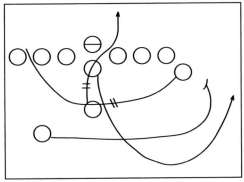

Diagram 2-18

The quarterback pivots to avoid the fullback's path. He brings the ball to the fullback's navel and either gives it to him or extracts it. He continues, as the wing comes to him. He either places the ball on the wing's navel or rubs the wing's navel with his open hand. He then continues the half-moon circle and either fakes the counter boot or executes the counter boot with the "run-first" philosophy.

❑ *The Counter Break from the Left-Fly Formation (Diagram 2-19):*

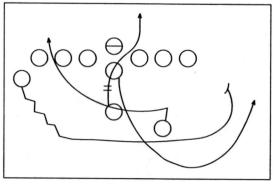

Diagram 2-19

- The actions of the fullback will not change from the right call.
- The halfback takes a large step toward the outside foot of the tight end, grabs grass with his outside hand, as he slides his inside foot up, and then cuts the half-moon path. He is now in the same position as from his wing path.
- The wing flies full speed on the one-count allowance and proceeds to get his wall-block position.

❑ *Counter Break from the Right-Double Call (Diagram 2-20)*

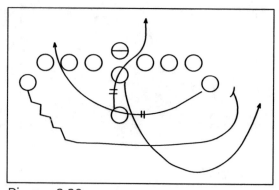

Diagram 2-20

- It is not necessary to practice the double-formation, since all of the techniques are already mastered on the other calls.

Coaching Point

    Repeat from the left call, the right-fly call, and the left-double call.

Fundamental Techniques for the Sweep Break

❑ *Right Formation (Diagram 2-21)*

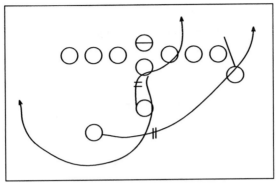

Diagram 2-21

- The fullback works on a wide-cut path through the outside foot of the guard.
- The halfback, taking a slight upward path, is given the ball on the sweep or takes a fake. If he gets the ball, he reads the blocking leverage by the kick man for the cut. If he does not get the ball, he sells the sweep.
- The quarterback opens as usual, for either a fullback-give or a fake. He continues to the halfback and will either gives the ball to the halfback and fakes the sweep boot or fakes the sweep and executes his boot with "run-first" philosophy.
- The wing blocks on the sweep and releases, after a block fake, on the bootleg.

❑ *Sweep Break on the Left-Fly Formation (Diagram 2-22)*

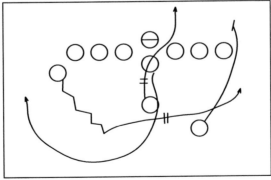

Diagram 2-22

- The actions of the fullback and the quarterback do not change from the right formation.

- The halfback either blocks at the outside foot of the tight end or fake-blocks and releases for the boot.
- The wing flies one count to his halfback position and then carries on the sweep or fakes the sweep on the boot play.

❑ *The Sweep Break on the Right-Double Formation (Diagram 2-23)*

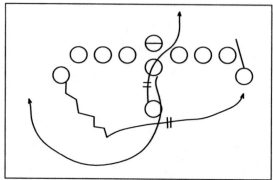

Diagram 2-23

- No need exists to practice the fundamentals on the double-call, since all of the attendant techniques are from the other formations and have already been practiced.

3

Blocking Schemes and Techniques

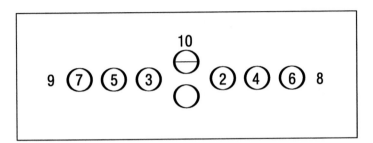

The player positions are numbered with even numbers to the right and odd numbers to the left. Guards are the 2 and 3 holes, tackles are the 4 and 5 holes, tight ends are the 6 and 7 holes, and the wide holes are 8 and 9. The right foot of the center is the 0 hole, while his left foot is the 1 hole. When plays are called, the last digit is the hole to be opened.

Two primary blocking schemes are utilized: the "POWER SCHEME" and the "DOWN SCHEME." If a block call is not added after the hole number, then the power scheme is automatically employed. If a blocking word is added to the play, then the blocking scheme is changed to that type. In other words, the power scheme is the basic blocking scheme, while the down scheme is the alternate. Some special letter and word calls can be used to change the blocking scheme.

The Power Scheme

❏ *The first downman inside of the hole called is double-teamed.*

- Hole man
  - ✓ Lead down on the downman on the first inside teammate.
  - ✓ If no downman is present, then block the first inside linebacker (BAB).
  - ✓ If there is no inside linebacker or if the defensive placement will not allow you to BAB (block across backer), then influence by either pulling and trap the first outside man or step up, make slight contact, and block away (SUBA).

- The first lineman inside of the hole called:
  - ✓ Post a downman on.
  - ✓ If no downman on, then lead down on the first downman inside.

- All other assignments are predetermined on each play. It may sound complicated, but it really isn't. Using the 7 hole ⍺ as an example (Diagrams 3-1, 3-2, 3-3, and 3-4), the straightforward application of the power scheme can be clearly seen.
  - ✓ vs. 52 (double-man on tackle); HOLE MAN—lead (Diagram 3-1)

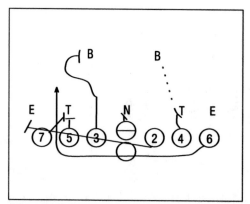

Diagram 3-1

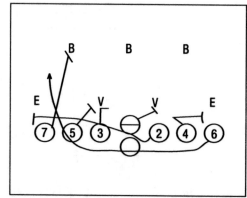

Diagram 3-2

  - ✓ vs. 43 (double-man on guard); HOLE MAN—BAB (Diagram 3-2)
  - ✓ vs. Split 4 (double-man on guard); HOLE MAN—BAB (Diagram 3-3)

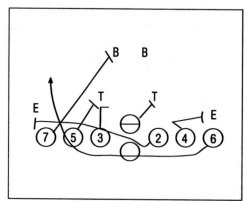

Diagram 3-3

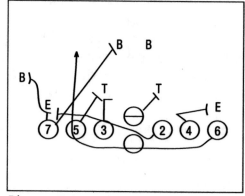

Diagram 3-4

  - ✓ vs. split 4; the defensive end will not allow the holeman to BAB, so the holeman will SUBA (step up, chip, and block away—influence). HOLEMAN—can't lead, can't BAB; so SUBA (Diagram 3-4).

The Down Scheme

❑ Certain kinds of defensive stunting and shooting by linebackers in the power scheme can be addressed by sealing and scooping. In some situations, however, the offense is forced to "break up the double" and go to the down scheme. The down scheme assignments are a simple block down on the first person inside. The 7 hole counter play can be used to illustrate the point (Diagrams 3-5 to 3-8).

• vs. 52 (Diagram 3-5)

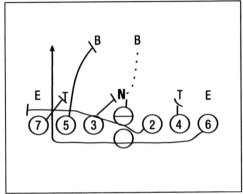

Diagram 3-5

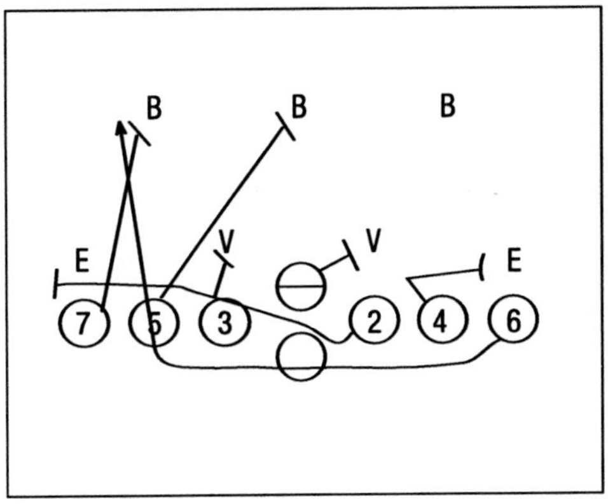

Diagram 3-6

• vs. 43; the playside guard will color call if he cannot block down on the middle linebacker (Diagram 3-6)
• vs. split (Diagram 3-7)
• vs. eagle (Diagram 3-8)

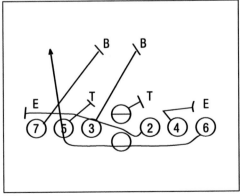

Diagram 3-7

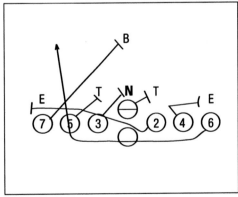

Diagram 3-8

❑ *Special Blocking Calls*

- G call—G refers to the word "George," which means it is a guard call (Diagram 3-9)

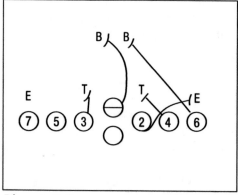

Diagram 3-9

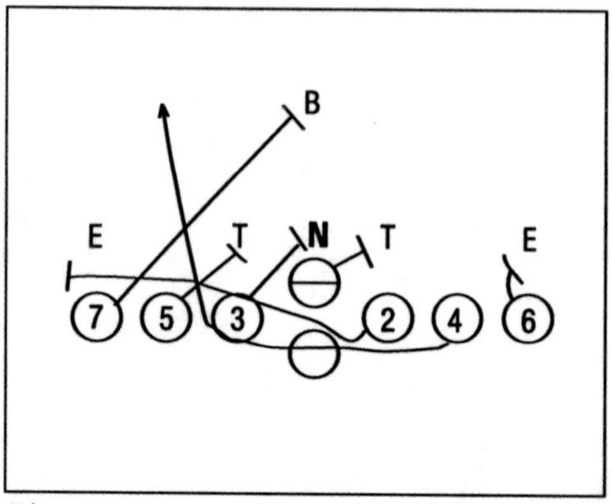

Diagram 3-10

- GT call—GT refers to George and Tom, when both the guard and the tackle are involved (Diagram 3-10)
- Fold call—on the base scheme, assignments are switched when the playside guard has a hardship block (Diagram 3-11)

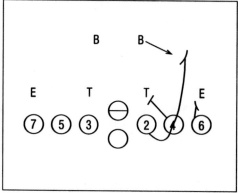

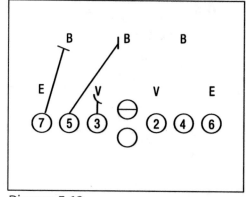

Diagram 3-11

Diagram 3-12

- Color call—on a down scheme, a color is called by the guard when he cannot block down (Diagram 3-12)

- S call—inside switch; the opposite of a fold call (Diagram 3-13)

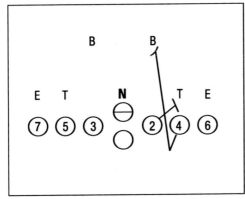

Diagram 3-13

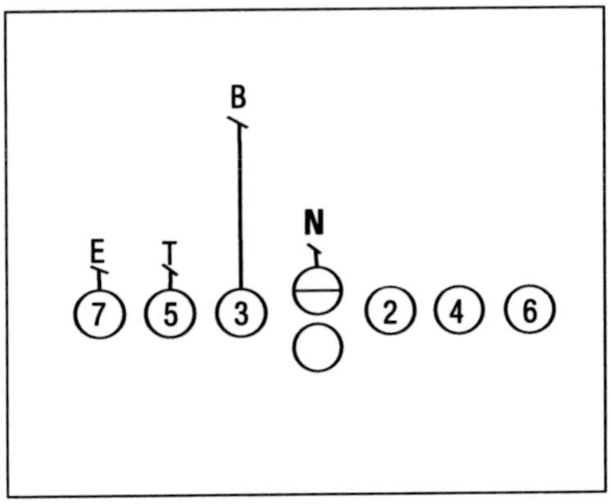

Diagram 3-14

- Base call—the offensive lineman blocks the man on him (Diagram 3-14)
- Zone call—enables the guard and tackle to pick up both the downman and the linebacker (Diagram 3-15)

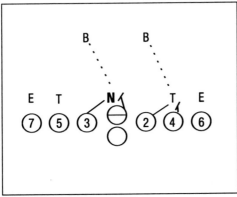

Diagram 3-15

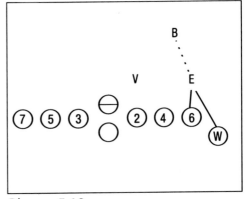

Diagram 3-16

- Combo call—enables the tight end and the wing to pick up both the downman and the linebacker; combo is the opposite of a zone call (Diagram 3-16)

Coaching Point

On a base call, the offensive lineman should block the man on him.

 • Base—inside, on, outside (Diagram 3-17):

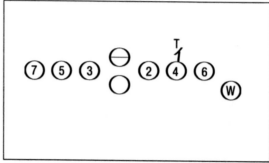

Diagram 3-17

The blocker should attain leverage on his initial contact, get his pads under his opponent, drive him off the line, finish him off with his hands, and "keep the glue" on him.

 • Post/lead—power block (Diagram 3-18):

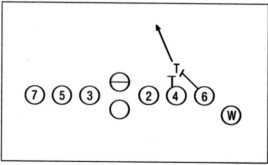

Diagram 3-18

 ✓ The post man (the inside man), employing the shoulder nearest the lead man, drives the defender upfield, using his shoulder and forearm with a neck lock to the inside.

 ✓ The lead man, employing the shoulder nearest the post man, drives the defender on a 45-degree angle inside, using a shoulder and forearm with a neck lock to the outside.

Coaching Point

Both blockers should get under the defender's pads, lift him up, and drive him 45 degrees inside, in an attempt to interfere with the defensive pursuit.

• Trap block—inside-out block (Diagram 3-19):

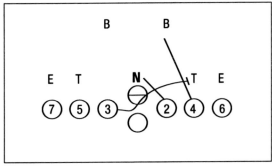

Diagram 3-19

The blocker jerks his inside arm hard, turns his inside foot parallel (he should not step), cross-over steps, and gets up in the hole. The blocker contacts the defender with his shoulders square to the sideline and employs leverage—getting under the defender's pads, driving him outside, then turning him deep.

Coaching Point

We believe that the hardest contact to be made in football is offensive contact, because the offensive player knows the snap count and knows exactly who he is going to hit before the snap.

• Kick block—blocking the contain man:
  ✓ The playside guard (Diagram 3-20)

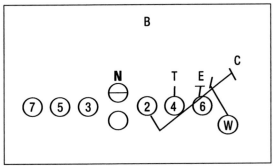

Diagram 3-20

The playside guard gets width and depth on his first step, then uses a crossover step, works up into the hole, and traps the contain man. If the contain man over-closes, the playside guard should log him by placing his leverage outside and basing him up.

✓ Fullback—on the 30 series (Diagram 3-21):

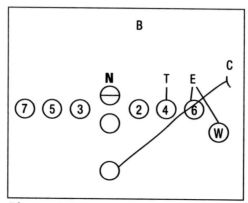

Diagram 3-21

The fullback gets the angle through the inside foot of the tight end, then works up into the hole to get a trap block. If the contain man over-closes, the fullback should place his leverage outside and base him up.

- Down block—the first opponent to inside:
  - ✓ The blocker uses his near-shoulder on a man who is not penetrating; principles of the lead block are followed (Diagram 3-22).

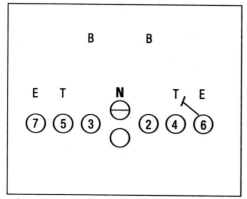

Diagram 3-22

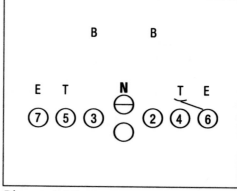

Diagram 3-23

✓ The blocker uses his far shoulder on a defender who is penetrating by placing his helmet under the defender's chest, then executes the far-shoulder contact, and drives down (Diagram 3-23).

- BAB block—block the first across linebacker (Diagram 3-24).

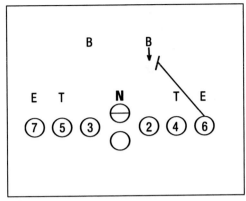

Diagram 3-24

The blocker takes a path through the hip of the tackle to meet the coming linebacker and employs the down-block fundamentals.

- Hands block—cut off the linebacker (Diagram 3-25):

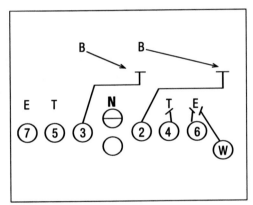

Diagram 3-25

- Assuming the correct position, the blocker takes the escape path. As soon as he is clear, he turns up toward the run lane, squares up, and locks up on the linebacker, using the hands block.

Coaching Point

To execute a BAB block, the blocker should take a path through the hip of the tackle to meet the on-coming linebacker and should employ down-block fundamentals.

- Escort block:
  - ✓ Tight end escort on the counter (Diagram 3-26). Stepping for width and depth, the tight end runs with his pads down. He keys the helmet of the trapping guard. If the guard's helmet is inside, the tight end squares up and gets through the hole with his eyes upfield. He takes inside first; his second choice is on; and his last choice is to take the outside.

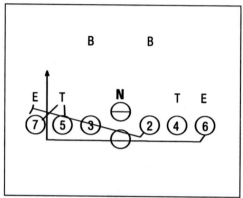

Diagram 3-26

  - ✓ Sweep escort by the off-guard (Diagram 3-27). The off-guard pulls, as if he is trapping. He must beat the fullback and get depth. He keys the playside guard's helmet. If his hat is inside, then the off-guard squares up, and gets through the hole (inside, on, outside). If the playside guard's helmet is outside, he then escorts outside.

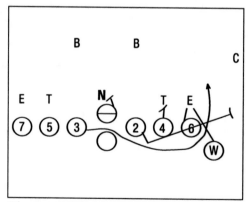

Diagram 3-27

- Seal block—closing the hole left by a pulling lineman, principally, on sweeps and sweep boots:

When sealing, the blocker turns his foot, crosses-over, lunges, and sprints his backside shoulder behind the butt of the second man over. Continuing to sprint, the seal blocker forces the defender to go either behind him or through him. The seal blocker does not allow the defender to cross his hat.

✓ Sealing the 52 (Diagram 3-28) ✓ Sealing the 43 (Diagram 3-29)

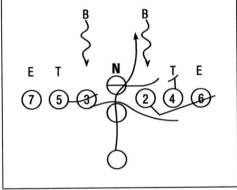

Diagram 3-28

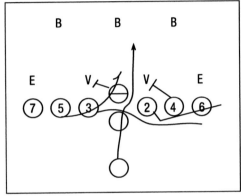

Diagram 3-29

✓ Sealing the split (Diagram 3-30) ✓ Sealing the eagle (Diagram 3-31)

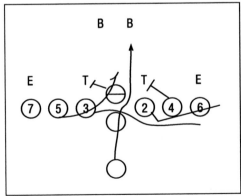

Diagram 3-30

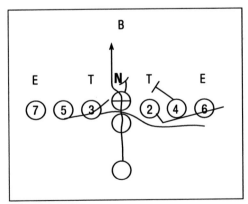

Diagram 3-31

• Reach block—outside, on, inside:

The reach block is employed when the wing or the halfback is asked to get outside leverage on the contain man. The blocker must sprint toward the sideline and get a square-up position on the contain man. The blocker then locks up with the contain man, and uses the "hands block" on the defender's chest for control. The blocker moves his feet laterally and keeps the "glue" on until help arrives.

✓ Reach block for the wing (Diagram 3-32)

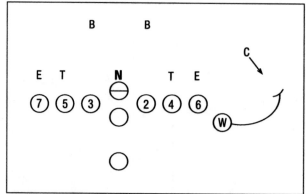

Diagram 3-32

✓ Reach block for the halfback (Diagram 3-33)

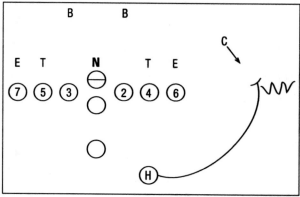

Diagram 3-33

- The wall block:
  - ✓ The halfback and the fly back employ a wall block on the counter boot. The halfback/wingback must sprint at full speed to get past the quarterback's path. They must key the first unblocked opponent. They get a position two yards outside of the defender and then, working in under control, lock the defender up, using the hands technique. The blocker's primary objective is to prevent the defender from getting to the quarterback's boot path (Diagrams 3-34 and 3-35).

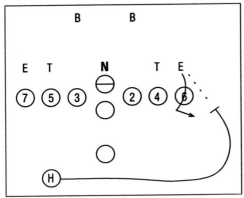

Diagram 3-34

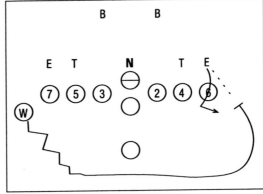

Diagram 3-35

  - ✓ The playside guard on the sweep boot. On the sweep boot, the playside guard is called the "wall guard." His job is to get an outside-in position on the first unblocked opponent and prevent him from going to the quarterback. The wall guard must pull deep in a circle path. He should be a full three yards deep at a point directly behind the tight end's pre-snap alignment. He must locate the defender and adjust his position until he can get his hands on the defender, lock him up, and keep him inside (Diagram 3-36).

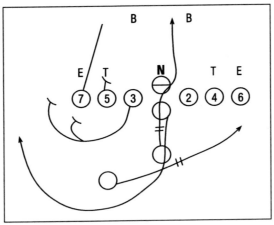

Diagram 3-36

- The fold block:

The fold block is a part of the base-blocking scheme. A fold block is used when a blocker is disadvantaged.

  ✓ The playside tackle must execute the down block quickly and must drive the man, so that the blocker's heels are clear of the guard's path on the fold.
  ✓ The playside guard is the fold man. On a fold block, he must take a large side step for depth and width and then cross over up into the hole, while keeping his shoulders parallel to the line. He must anticipate the movement of the linebacker and move to a lock-up position, using the hands technique in order to gain some degree of outside leverage (Diagram 3-37).

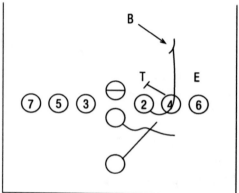 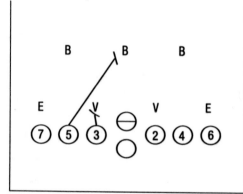

Diagram 3-37   Diagram 3-38

- The color block:

In a down blocking scheme, a few defensive alignments can pose a disadvantage for a blocker, for example:

  ✓ The playside guard is disadvantaged, because he may not be able to down block the middle linebacker on the 43 alignment. As a result, he should call a color to his tackle and switch assignments. In this situation, the guard has base, while the tackle has the linebacker (Diagram 3-38).
  ✓ On a color call, the playside tackle blocks the playside guard's man, instead of blocking down.

Staff Assignments

Teaching and implementing the mis-direction wing-T with multi-points of attack offense can be handled with coaching staffs of various sizes. Ideally, a four-man staff is appropriate, although the task can be handled by either a three-man or a two-man staff. Using Diagram 4-1 as a means to specify the various positions, the staff assignments are detailed in the following sub-sections:

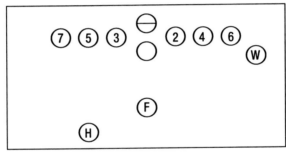

Diagram 4-1

❑ *A Four-Man Staff*
- Phase #1 staff breakdown:
  ✓ Interior line (1-5)
  ✓ Tight ends (6, 7)
  ✓ Halfback and wing (H, W)
  ✓ Quarterbacks and fullbacks (Q, F)
- Phase #2 staff breakdown:
  ✓ Centers and guards—interior coach
  ✓ Tackles and tight ends—tight ends coach works the integration between the tackles and tight ends
  ✓ Backfield group—quarterbacks and fullbacks coach and halfbacks and wings coach

- Phase #3 staff breakdown:
  - ✓ Front seven—interior coach and tight ends coach
  - ✓ Backfield group—continue as for phase #2
- Phase #4 staff breakdown:
  - ✓ Centers, guards and tackles—interior coach
  - ✓ Tight ends and backfield—blocking coordination between halfbacks, wings, and tight ends; the pass attack
- Phase #5 teamwork:
  - ✓ The tight ends coach handles the scout defense and coaches the tight ends.

❑ *A Three-Man Staff*

- The line coach can handle the entire front seven nicely, due to the double-tight situation.
- The backfield group is staffed the same as for the four-man staff. One coach serves as a halfback/wingback coach, while a second coach takes the quarterback and the fullback.
- In teamwork sessions, the halfback/wingback coach takes the scout team, while the quarterback/fullback coach handles the backfield.

❑ *A Two-Man Staff*

- One coach handles the front seven, while another coach is in charge of the backfield.
- A two-man staff is often particularly suitable for small high schools and/or junior varsity and freshmen level programs.

5

Play Selection

A bad play cannot be called in this offensive system, as long as the play-caller adheres to the principle of "keep 'em mixed thoroughly." The key point to remember is that the play-caller must not establish tendencies on which his opponents can feed. Among the personnel who are responsible for helping select and send a play into the game are the following:

- If sufficient personnel are available, two individuals involved in play selection are located in the press box—a play-caller and a spotter. The play-caller should be the line coach. He should work closely with a press-box spotter, who should observe the defense and its reactions, changes, and tendencies. The press-box spotter should chart this information and pass it along to the play-caller as expeditiously as possible.
- The sideline-phone man should get the play to the quarterback in a timely fashion, via messenger or signal.
- The sideline-chart man should record the formation, the play, the down-and-distance, the field position, and the result.
- The "take-off coach" is responsible for getting players out of their stances on the snap. He should note all 11 hats and motivate those who are even a hair late. The snap count should start a "feeding frenzy" on the part of the offense.

Coaching Point

The play-caller must not establish tendencies on which his opponent can feed.

At least six guidelines should affect a coach's philosophy of selecting plays:

- Mix the plays and the formations in all situations of down and distance and field position.
- Do not "fall in love" immediately with a play that gains well.
- Do not file divorce proceedings on a play that does not gain.
- Mix flies equally and mix formations equally; furthermore, mix formations and flies to the wide and short sides of a field equally.
- Remember that boots and counters are excellent short-yardage and goal-line calls, as long as a team has established the philosophy of "run first" on boots.
- Mix run and pass in both short-yardage situations and long-yardage situations.

PART II:
THE PACKAGES

©Kenny Felt/ICON SMI

Introduction to the "Packages" Section

Note: All plays are diagrammed to the right only. In order to be seen to the left, they must be flipped.

❑ *Right Formations:*
  • Right (Diagram PII-1):

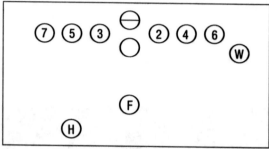

Diagram PII-1

  • Left-fly (Diagram PII-2):

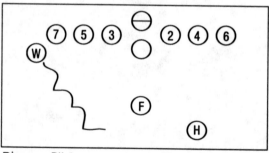

Diagram PII-2

  • Right-double (Diagram PII-3):

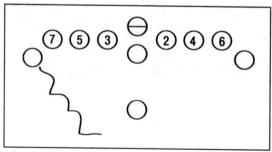

Diagram PII-3

❑ *All plays against the 52 defense are diagrammed first and then carried on through the 43, the split, and the eagle.*

• The 52 defensive alignment (Diagram PII-4):

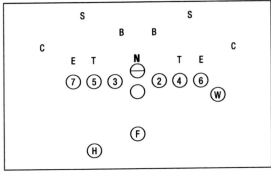

Diagram PII-4

• The 43 defensive alignment (Diagram PII-5):

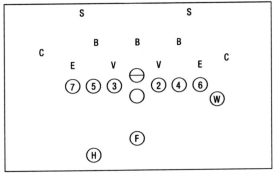

Diagram PII-5

• The split defensive alignment (Diagram PII-6):

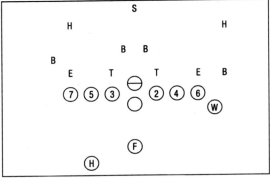

Diagram PII-6

• The eagle defensive alignment (Diagram PII-7):

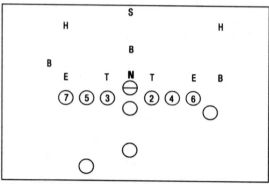

Diagram PII-7

6

The Fullback Package

In the three points of attack concept, the fullback is the focal point. Given the fact that the fundamental philosophical basis of the mis-direction wing-T with multi-points of attack offense is to control pursuit, then the middle attack must be emphasized. This approach forces the defense to "check-and-take or eliminate" the fullback on every snap. The fullback must cover and conceal the ball with both arms, until he clears the linebackers. When the fullback is faking, he must proceed, exactly, as if he has the ball. He must "sell the carry" to the defense. The fullback package is the backbone of the mis-direction offense and is the primary reason that the remainder of the attack is able to produce excellent results.

All factors considered, a small, quick fullback is preferred for the fullback package. A small fullback needs less of a running lane crease. The blocking ability of the fullback is last on our list of essential attributes for a fullback.

Position Symbols	
C	The Center
PG	Playside Guard
BG	Backside Guard
PT	Playside Tackle
BT	Backside Tackle
PE	Playside Tight End
BE	Backside Tight End
FB	Fullback
HB	Halfback
WB	Wingback
QB	Quarterback

Blocking Rules

❑ *22 Trap*

- Right 22 trap vs. the 52 defense (Diagram 6-1)

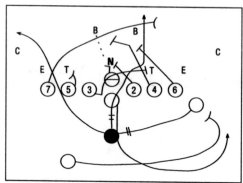

Diagram 6-1

PG (Hole called) lead, BAB, SUBA/influence
PT BAB/combo
PE BAB (block across backer)
C   Away, post
BG Trap first down man past the center
BT Base, linebacker
BE BAH (block across hole)
FB Dive, receive ball, cover ball, cut behind trapper, get around the BAB and upfield; make the trapper hurry
LH Get wall position on first unblocked for cx boot
WB Fake counter carry; sell it
QB Give to FB; sell counter; sell counter boot

- Left fly 22 trap vs. the 43 defense (Diagram 6-2)

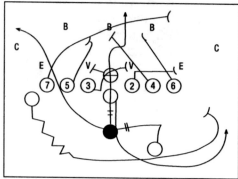

Diagram 6-2

• Right double 22 trap vs. the split defense (Diagram 6-3)

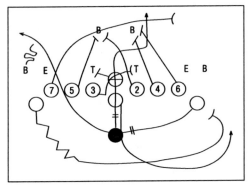

Diagram 6-3

• Right 22 trap vs. the eagle defense (Diagram 6-4)

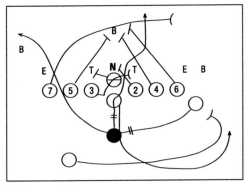

Diagram 6-4

Coaching Point

Given the fact that the fundamental philosophical basis of the mis-direction wing-T with multi-points of attack offense is to control pursuit, then the middle attack must be emphasized.

❑ *Special Fullback Plays vs. the 52 Defense*
  • 22 dive (Diagram 6-5)

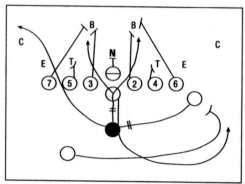

Diagram 6-5

PG	Base	BT	Base
PT	Base	BE	BAB
PE	BAB	FB	Key nose man's helmet; take
C	Base the nose man the way		the ball and cut away from
	he wants to go.		the nose man's helmet.
BG	Base	Others	Same as 22 trap

  • 22 dive double S vs. the 52 defense (Diagram 6-6)

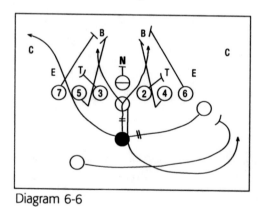

Diagram 6-6

PG	Block out; drive him out quickly.	BG	Block out; drive him out quickly.
PT	Step in and get up on linebacker.	BT	Step in and get up on linebacker.
PE	BAB	BE	BAB
C	Same as dive.	Others	Same as 22 dive.

• 22 dive SOS—SOS means that the guards step out to the sideline (Diagram 6-7)

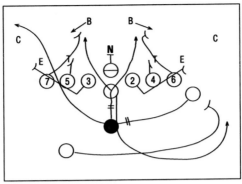

Diagram 6-7

PG	Pull out and trap the defensive end.		BG	Pull out and trap the defensive end.
PT	Base		BT	Base
PE	Dig the linebacker.		BE	Dig the linebacker.
C	Same as 22 dive.		Others	Same as 22 dive.

• 22 trap "backdoor" vs. the 52 defense (Diagram 6-8)

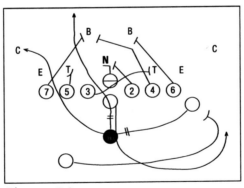

Diagram 6-8

All assignments are the same as 22 trap except:

BE	BAB
FB	Take ball and cut away from the hole.
BT	Has the key block; keep the hole open.

❏ *22 Trap-Toss*

• Right 22 trap-toss vs. the
  52 defense (Diagram 6-9)

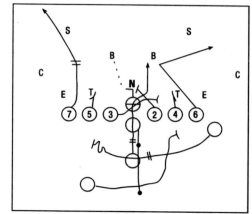

Diagram 6-9

PG Lead
PT Base, out
PE BAB, lets the LB hit him,
    breaks out to daylight.
C   Away, base
BG Trap the #2 area.
BT Base, out
BE Escape step, upfield looking for toss at five yards; if the QB "pumps," break
    to flag, looking for ball outside.
FB Super fake the 22 trap; run into the linebacker.
HB Wall path, break up to block the DE.
WB Counter path, break and block the DE.
QB Take ball to the FB, pop the ball to the BE at five yards deep. If he is
    covered, pump and drop and look from the BE to the PE for "feed off."

Coaching Point

The trap-toss controls the backside linebacker.

• Left fly 22 trap-toss vs. the
  43 defense (Diagram 6-10)

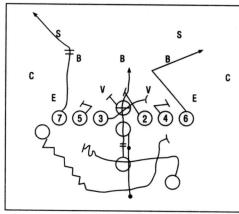

Diagram 6-10

> On the 22 trap-toss play, the wing back takes a counter path, breaks, and blocks the defensive end.

- Right double 22 trap-toss vs. the split defense (Diagram 6-11)

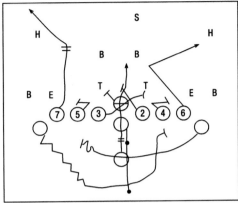

Diagram 6-11

- Right 22 trap-toss vs. the eagle defense (Diagram 6-12)

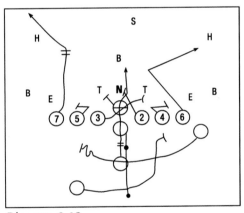

Diagram 6-12

Coaching Point ───────────────────────────────

> If 22 trap-toss "PUMP" is called in the huddle, the toss is faked.

Coaching Point

On 22 trap-toss, the fullback should execute a super fake for the 22 trap, and then run into the linebacker.

❑ *29 Shoot*

This play is designed to control the defense to the tight end/halfback side of the formation.

• Right 29 shoot vs. the 52 defense (Diagram 6-13)

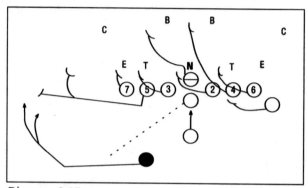

Diagram 6-13

PE	Base	BE	Scoop
PT	Pull at full speed, slightly upfield toward the sideline; reach-block the contain man or wall him out into the sideline.	WB	Scoop
		QB	Get the ball to the HB right now.
		HB	Sprint flat full speed until the ball arrives; do not wait for the ball; stretch the defense; cut daylight.
PB	Scoop		
C	Scoop		
BG	Scoop	FB	Fake the dive.
BT	Scoop		

Coaching Point

The 29 shoot play is called when the tight end can base block the defender on him and the contain man is off the line of scrimmage.

• 29 shoot vs. the 43 defense (Diagram 6-14)

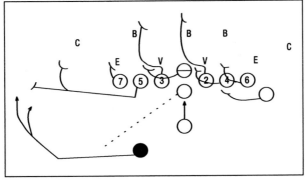

Diagram 6-14

• 29 shoot vs. the split defense (Diagram 6-15)

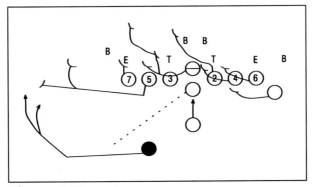

Diagram 6-15

• 29 shoot vs. the eagle defense (Diagram 6-16)

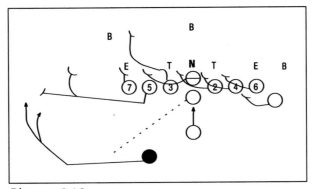

Diagram 6-16

❑ *22 Trap Shoot-Toss*

• Right 22 trap shoot-toss vs. the 52 defense (Diagram 6-17)

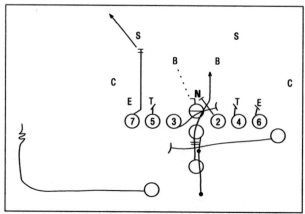

Diagram 6-17

All assignments are the same as for the 22 trap-toss except:

HB   Shoot out until a point 12 yards wide is reached, then turn up and hang just behind the line of scrimmage.

QB   Sell the trap, hit the TE if open; if not, drop and check flat and flag.

WB   Block the backside DE.

Coaching Point

The toss to the TE is still the number one choice.

• Right 22 trap shoot-toss vs. the 43 defense (Diagram 6-18)

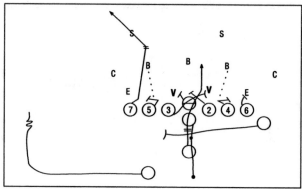

Diagram 6-18

Coaching Point

On 22 trap shoot-toss, the halfback should shoot laterally for 12 yards, then turn up, and hang just behind the line of scrimmage.

• Right 22 trap shoot-toss vs. the split defense (Diagram 6-19)

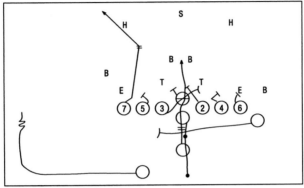

Diagram 6-19

• Right 22 trap shoot-toss vs. the eagle defense (Diagram 6-20)

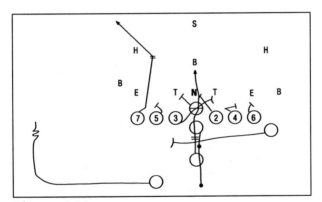

Diagram 6-20

Coaching Point

On 22 trap toss, the quarterback should sell the trap and hit the tight end if he's open; if not, he should drop and check the flat and flag.

❏ *Shoot 23 Trap*

    • Right shoot 23 trap vs. the 52 defense (Diagram 6-21)

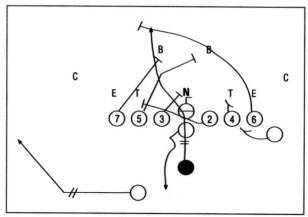

Diagram 6-21

All assignments are the same as for the 23 trap except the backfield action.

Coaching Point

    Fake the shoot and run the trap to the side of the shoot action; keep in mind that some linebackers like to run to shoot action.

Some linebackers like to run to shoot action.

• Right shoot 23 trap vs. the 43 defense (Diagram 6-22)

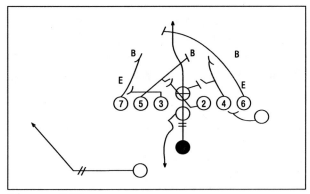

Diagram 6-22

• Right shoot 23 trap vs. the split defense (Diagram 6-23)

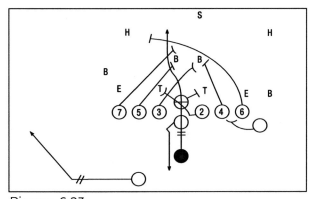

Diagram 6-23

• Right shoot 23 trap vs. the eagle defense (Diagram 6-24)

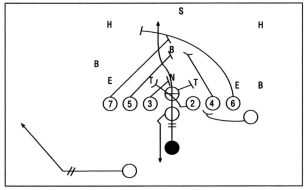

Diagram 6-24

❏ *24 Trap Down*

This play is the "wide" fullback trap, in which the 4 and 5 hole traps are always out of the sweep break, in order to influence the outside portion of the defense and to keep them from compressing.

• Right 24 trap vs. the 52 defense—reverts to the 2 hole, if the playside guard is uncovered (Diagram 6-25):

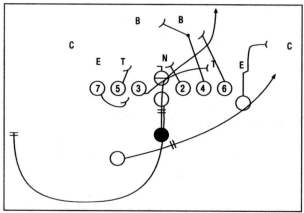

Diagram 6-25

PT	(Hole called) down	FB	Same steps as in 22 trap,
PG	Down (make color call for switch with the PT if necessary).		except make a sharp cut to get around the down block on the defender on the PG.
PE	BAB	QB	Give the ball to the FB; sell
C	Away		the sweep; sell the sweep
BG	Trap first down man past the PG.		boot.
		HB	Sell the sweep.
BT	Scoop, seal the ball.	WB	Influence/chip the DE and
BE	Scoop, seal the PT hole.		wall out the contain man.

Coaching Point

The down blocking scheme is always called on the 24 and 25 traps. If the 24 trap is called and the defense shows up in the 52, then the 2 hole trap is automatically executed.

• Left-fly 24 trap vs. the 43 defense (Diagram 6-26)

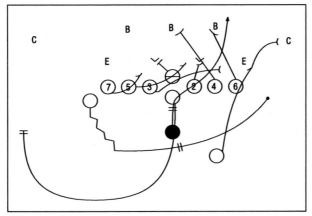

Diagram 6-26

Coaching Point

A color call should be made by the playside guard, since he cannot down block the middle linebacker.

• Right double 24 trap vs. the split defense (Diagram 6-27)

• Right 24 trap vs. the eagle defense (Diagram 6-28)

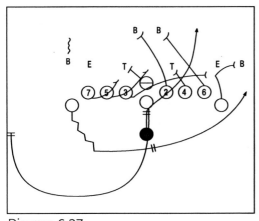

Diagram 6-27

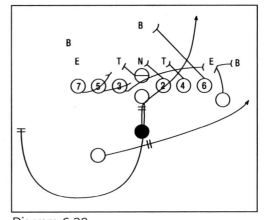

Diagram 6-28

7

The Counter (CX) Package

The counters were our leading average per-carry plays. Statistically, the counters were second on the list of most called plays, with the fullback trap being first. The counter has produced positive results in all situations of down, yardage, and field position, including the "red zone" and the goal line. The counter play to the left has always out-gained the one to the right. In all likelihood, this situation is either the result of the blockers' right-handedness or dominant side or a by-product of the strongside placement of defensive personnel to the right.

In the mis-direction wing-T offense, the counter is a "basic" play, whereas in most offenses it is an occasional play. Frankly, the mis-direction wing-T offense involves more counter plays than almost any modern offense, although it appears that many of the current one-back offenses are countering more than ever before.

©Kenny Felt/ICON SMI

• Right 27 counter vs. the 52 defense (Diagram 7-1)

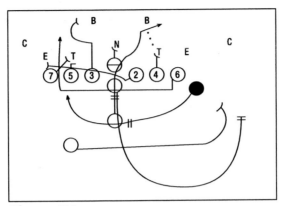

Diagram 7-1

PE	Lead, BAB SUBA (hole called).
PT	Post, lead
PG	Base
C	Base, away
BG	Trap or log first color.
BT	Seal, base
BE	Escort through hole; read the hat of the trapper to cut up or go wide.
FB	Sell the trap.
HB	Fake the wall block.
QB	Sell the fullback trap; give to counter back; sell the counter boot.
WB	Catch the escort man; read trapper's hat for cut.

• Left fly 27 counter vs. the 43 defense (Diagram 7-2)

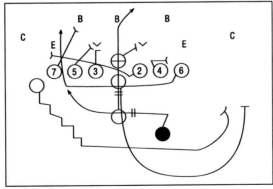

Diagram 7-2

• Right double 27 counter vs. the split defense (Diagram 7-3)

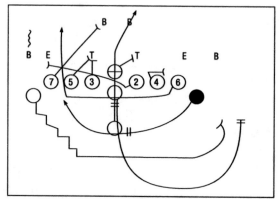

Diagram 7-3

• Right 27 counter vs. the eagle defense (Diagram 7-4)

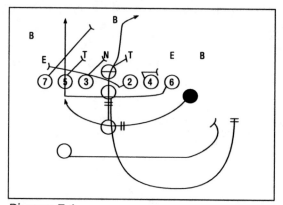

Diagram 7-4

Points of Emphasis for Teaching the Counter

❑ *Holeman Blocking Rule Progression*
  • Lead, when the tackle is covered (Diagram 7-5)

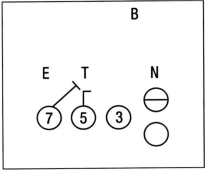

Diagram 7-5

  • BAB, when the tackle is uncovered (Diagram 7-6)

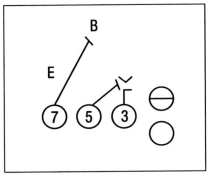

Diagram 7-6

  • SUBA, when the defensive alignment will not allow a BAB (Diagram 7-7)

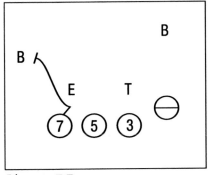

Diagram 7-7

The huddle call is "right 27 cx down."

• Down call vs. the 52 defense—actually a pair of zone blocks (Diagram 7-8)

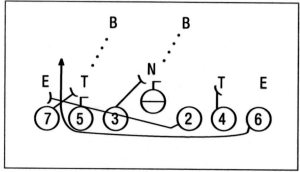

Diagram 7-8

• Down call vs. the 43 defense. The PG makes a color call to the PT.

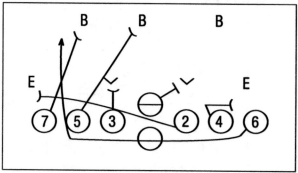

Diagram 7-9

• Down call vs. the split defense (Diagram 7-10)

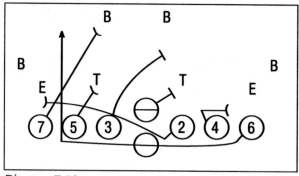

Diagram 7-10

- Down call vs. the eagle defense. SUBA is shown when the DE will not allow a BAB by either the PE or the hole man (Diagram 7-11).

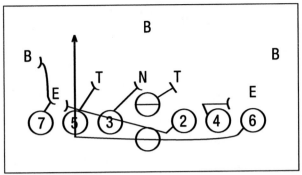

Diagram 7-11

- The offense goes to the down scheme when the seal blocks are not successful and when the defense presents major blitzing.

- If the defensive end chases the counter successfully, then the 30 series on the counter is called and plugs the DE with the fullback. The chase of the counter has never been a major problem, since we are extremely quick on the count, and we get in the hole right now and attempt to "catch" the escort man (Diagram 7-12).

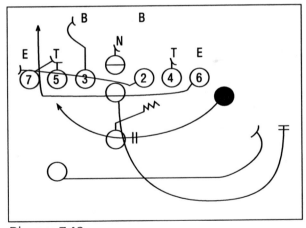

Diagram 7-12

Coaching Point

On the 27 counter play, if the defensive end chases the counter successfully, then the 30 series on the counter is called an plugs the defensive end with the fullback.

❑ *The 27 Counter Lateral Call*

The purpose of this call is to prevent the closing nature by the defensive end and the contain man. The call is designed to draw the defense in to the counter and then pitch the ball outside.

• Right 27 counter lateral vs. the 52 defense (Diagram 7-13)

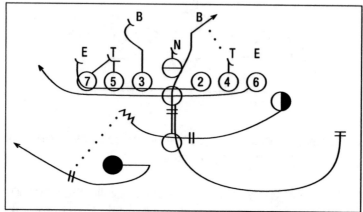

Diagram 7-13

The blocking schemes are the same as for the 27 counter except:

BG	Always log the DE.
BE	Escort the play wide.
CX Back	Runs the counter until he approaches the playside tackle, then, breaks down his feet and makes a controlled pitch.
HB	Turns the inside foot and takes two steps, plants, and faces the line, as he pivots back for depth. He gets a lateral position and "hangs" until the ball is pitched. He carries the ball with "wide" intent, while reading the block of the escort man.

Coaching Points

✓ *The offense also calls a "base scheme."*

✓ *If the offense feels that the backside defensive end will chase and interfere, then this play is run, using the 30 series, and the DE is plugged with the fullback.*

• Left fly 27 counter lateral vs. 43 defense (Diagram 7-14)

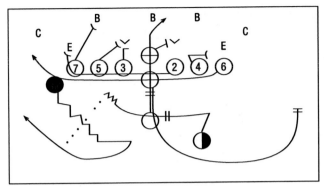

Diagram 7-14

• Right double 27 counter lateral vs. the split defense (Diagram 7-15)

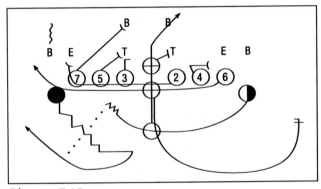

Diagram 7-15

• Right 27 counter lateral vs. the eagle defense—the down call is preferred vs. the eagle (Diagram 7-16)

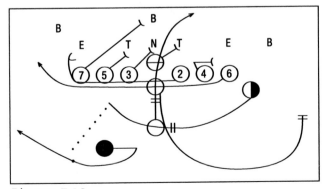

Diagram 7-16

❏ *The GT (Guard and Tackle) Call on the Counter Play*

The GT call can be added to the down scheme. When that occurs, the GT is run from the 30 series to avoid the "conflict" between the fullback and the pulling tackle.
  • Right 37 counter down GT vs. the 52 defense (Diagram 7-17)

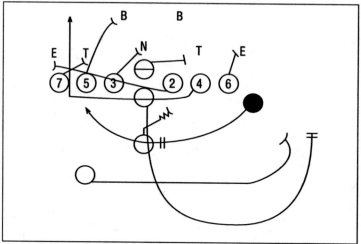

Diagram 7-17

  • Left fly 37 counter down GT vs. the 43 defense (Diagram 7-18)

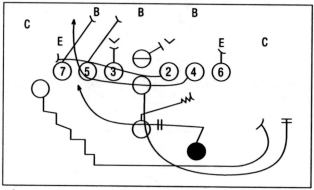

Diagram 7-18

Coaching Point

  When a GT call is added to the counter play, the crossing back runs the counter and follows the playside tackle through the hole.

• Right double 37 counter down GT vs. the split defense (Diagram 7-19)

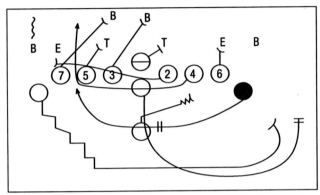

Diagram 7-19

• Right 37 counter down GT vs. the eagle defense (Diagram 7-20)

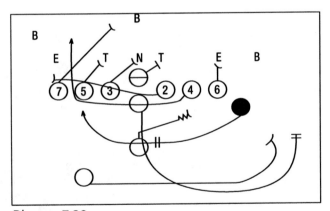

Diagram 7-20

❏ *The "TOM" Call*

This call on the counter play means that the tackle should be the trapper, and the playside guard should block away on the down scheme. This call is very effective against stunting and blitzing defenses.

• Right 37 counter down Tom vs. the 52 defense (Diagram 7-21)

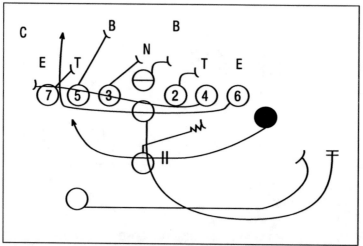

Diagram 7-21

On a "TOM" call on a counter play, the tackle should be the trapper.

• Left fly 37 counter down Tom vs. the 43 defense (Diagram 7-22)

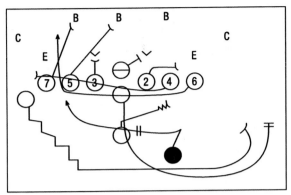

Diagram 7-22

• Right double 37 counter down Tom vs. the split defense (Diagram 7-23)

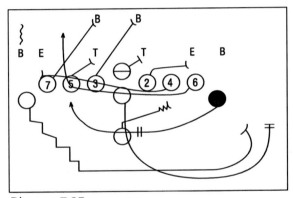

Diagram 7-23

• Right 37 counter down Tom vs. the eagle defense (Diagram 7-24)

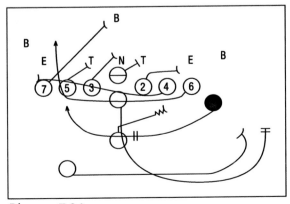

Diagram 7-24

❏ *The Counter Criss Cross (CXX) Call*

The CXX is a double handoff that is designed to influence the defense. If the defensive end's assignment is to check the quarterback on the sweep-boot action, then his movement outside will open the counter hole.

• Right 37 counter criss cross call vs. the 52 defense (Diagram 7-25)

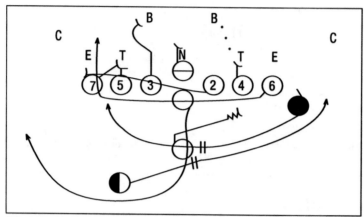

Diagram 7-25

All assignments are the same except:

QB	Hands off to the sweep back as soon as possible and then fakes the sweep boot action.
FB	Executes 30 series and plugs first unblocked color.
HB	Controls his speed without "giving a clue." Receives the ball from the QB and gives the ball to the Wing. Then, fakes the sweep carry.
WB	Jabs up on his outside foot and then gets on his counter path, comes to the HB, receives the ball and runs the counter hole.

Coaching Point

It is not necessary, at this point, to diagram the counter criss cross against all defenses, since it involves the same counter blocking assignments, and the DE is plugged with the fullback.

Since the wingbacks have already learned to pitch the ball on the counter lateral, it is very easy to run a counter criss cross-lateral play, which places extreme pressure on the defense if the defenders gather to stop the counter criss cross (Diagram 7-26).

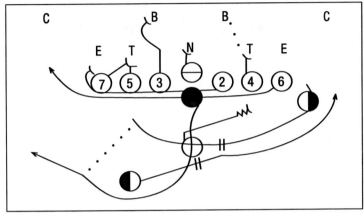

Diagram 7-26

All assignments remain the same as in counter lateral except:

QB   After the sweep hand off, get into a lateral position for the pitch and hang until the ball is released.

HB   Execute the CXX play.

8

The Counter Boot Package

Properly executing all fakes and the "run-first" philosophy of the quarterback are the keys that make the counter boot package effective as a third threat on the "mis-direction three points of attack" offensive style. Similar to other parts of the mis-direction wing-T offense, the formations and actions of the counter-boot package must be fully mixed on all counter boot calls. In other words, counter boots must be mixed into the play-selection procedure and in all situations of field width and depth, as well as in all down-and-yardage situations to gain positioning.

©Elsburgh Clarke Photography

❏ *The 20 Counter Boot*

• Right 27 counter boot vs. the 52 defense (Diagram 8-1)

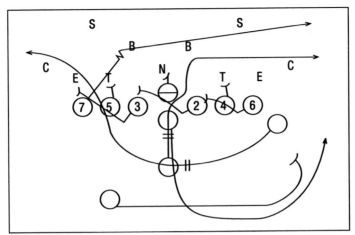

Diagram 8-1

C	Base, seal to the ball as he checks the linebacker.
PG	Trap opposite guard hole.
PT	Base, down
PE	Influence pull and trap first color to show.
BG	Trap the defensive end.
BT	Base (in gap, on, outside)
BE	Fake the BAB; release to daylight across the field.
QB	Sell the fullback trap, sell the counter, and then boot the ball wide. Attack the line of scrimmage and run. The QB has the option of throwing, if a receiver is open and if the QB feels he can get the ball to him.
FB	Sell the trap for five yards, and then sprint to the sideline.
HB	Get wall position on the first color to show.
CX Back	Sell the counter fully; check the throwback coverage.

Coaching Point

On the 20 counter boot play, the fullback should set the trap for five yards and then sprint to the sideline.

• Left fly 27 counter boot vs. the 43 defense (Diagram 8-2)

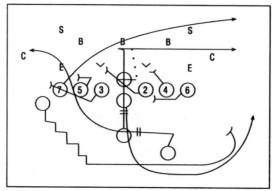

Diagram 8-2

• Right double 27 counter boot vs. the split defense (Diagram 8-3)

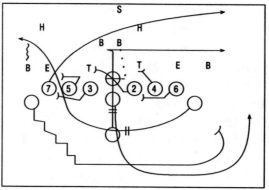

Diagram 8-3

• Right 27 counter boot vs. the eagle defense (Diagram 8-4)

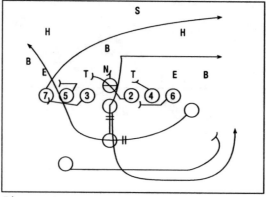

Diagram 8-4

This call gives the offense more receivers but less faking. It is usually effective due to the flooding of the three receivers and the throwback possibility.

• Right 37 counter boot vs. the 52 defense (Diagram 8-5)

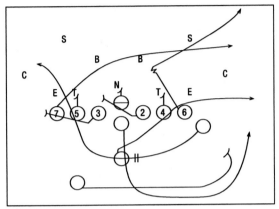

Diagram 8-5

All assignments are the same as the 20 series except:

PE   Fake the BAB and break the flag angle.
BE   Fake BAB and cross at 15.
FB   Step up on the opposite foot, and then find a way to get into the flat no deeper than five yards.
QB   The same as for the 20 series and the reminder of the "run-first" philosophy.

• Left fly 37 counter boot vs. the 43 defense (Diagram 8-6)

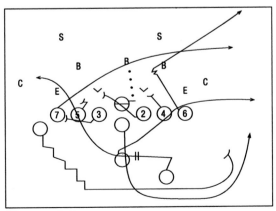

Diagram 8-6

• Right double 37 counter boot vs. the split defense (Diagram 8-7)

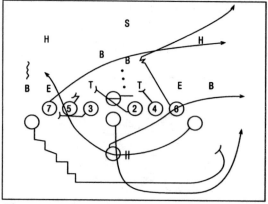

Diagram 8-7

• Right 37 counter boot vs. the eagle defense (Diagram 8-8)

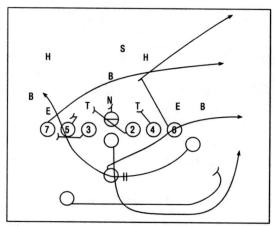

Diagram 8-8

Coaching Point

On a 30 series counter boot ball, the fullback should step up on his opposite foot and then find a way to get into the flat no deeper than five yards.

❑ *The 37 Counter Boot Throwback Call*

The coaches in the press box should note the defensive reaction to the counter back during the running of the counter boot. If the defense is not covering the counter back or if it is not covering him in certain areas, then the counter-boot throwback should be executed, because the counter back is wide open.

• Right 37 counter boot throwback vs. 52 defense (Diagram 8-9)

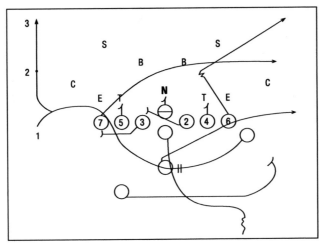

Diagram 8-9

All assignments are the same as for 37 counter boot except:

Counter Back	Fake the counter, but make a "poor" one to show the defenders that he definitely does not have the ball; get into the position for the throwback as called.

       ✓ If a 1 pattern is called, get on the line of scrimmage 10 yards wide and face the QB.

       ✓ If a 2 pattern is called, turn upfield after 10 yards and hang at 7-to-10 yards.

       ✓ If a 3 pattern is called, run a 2 pattern, but fly deep.

QB	Check the flood receivers and "pump" the ball, and then hit the throwback man as called.

• Left fly 37 counter boot throwback vs. 4-3 defense (Diagram 8-10)

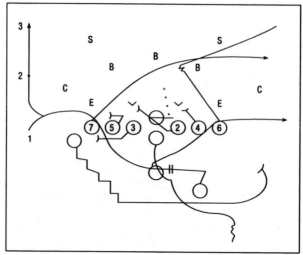

Diagram 8-10

• Right double 37 counter boot throwback vs. split defense (Diagram 8-11)

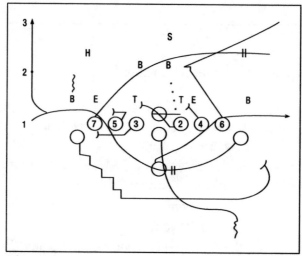

Diagram 8-11

Coaching Point

On the 37 counter boot throwback, the quarterback should check the flood receivers, "pump" the ball, and then hit the throwback man as called.

9

The Sweep Package

The "sweep break," which was previously discussed in Chapter 2, is designed to carry out the "three points of attack philosophy" by presenting the sweep, the fullback trap, and the sweep boot at each snap. These three plays should be called an equal number of times, to the extent possible during the game, in order to influence the pursuit of the defense. The mixture of the three formations to each side—the right and left formations, the left and right fly formations, and the right and left double formations—should be employed equally. In addition, the sweeps and the sweep boots should be run to both the wide side of the field and the short side of the field.

The backs who are not getting the ball must carry out "super" fakes, fully up the field. The fullback must "hide" the ball as long as possible. The quarterback must be skilled on the fake and the carry. The sweep back must cover the ball as he shifts it to his carrying pocket, and he must employ super faking when he's not carrying the ball.

©Mark Faram

❑ *The 20 Series Sweep (28 and 29)*

 • Right 28 sweep vs. the 52 defense (Diagram 9-1)

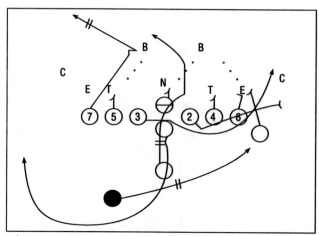

Diagram 9-1

PE	Combo block the defensive end, along with the wing.
WB	Combo block the man on the tight end. Apply the BAB rule if this man aligns inside on the tight end.
PT	Base, down
PG	Trap or log the first man outside of the wing.
C	Seal, base
BG	Escort through the hole. Read the PG's hat for trap/log.
BT	Seal, base
BE	Fake BAB, break to the flag, "asking" for the pass.
QB	Sell the trap, give the ball to the sweep back, and fake the sweep boot fully.
FB	Sell the trap; plug into any threat and get upfield.
Sweepback	Come to QB slightly, get the ball and read PG's hat for the cut.

Coaching Point ————————————————————

   On the 20 series sweep, the quarterback should sell the trap, give the ball to the sweep back, and fake the sweep boot fully.

On the 20 series sweep, the playside end should combo block the defensive end, along with the wing back.

- Left fly 28 sweep vs. the 43 defense (Diagram 9-2)

- Right double 28 sweep vs. the split defense (Diagram 9-3)

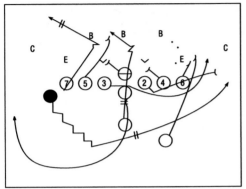

Diagram 9-2

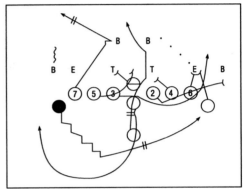

Diagram 9-3

- Right 28 sweep vs. the eagle defense (Diagram 9-4)

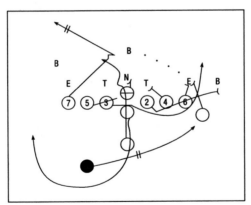

Diagram 9-4

The tight end and the wingback perform a combo block. The tight end and wing drive the man who aligns on the tight end up the field, while reading the first inside linebacker. If the linebacker comes to the inside, then the tight end will come off on him. If the linebacker moves outside, then the wing will pick him up.

- Combo block vs. 52
  (Diagram 9-5)

- Combo block vs. 43
  (Diagram 9-6)

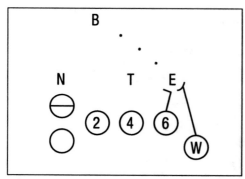

Diagram 9-5

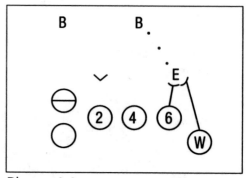

Diagram 9-6

- Combo block vs. split
  (Diagram 9-7)

- Combo block vs. eagle
  (Diagram 9-8)

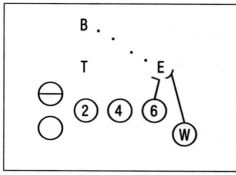

Diagram 9-7

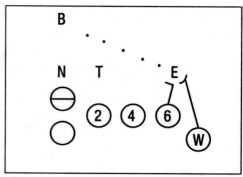

Diagram 9-8

- Combo block vs. 8-man front defensive end who aligns to take inside leverage; the wing applies his BAB rule (Diagram 9-9).

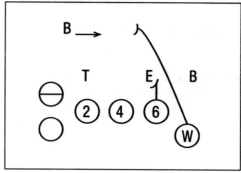

Diagram 9-9

This call means that the playside guard base blocks, while the fullback becomes the trap/log man. Although the play involves losing the fake to the fullback on the sweep, the offense gains a base blocker to the playside, in case it is getting pressure through the playside guard's pull hole. All other assignments remain the same, except for the playside guard and the fullback. In addition, the center's rule changes, since the playside guard is not pulling.

• Right 38 sweep vs. the 52 defense (Diagram 9-10)

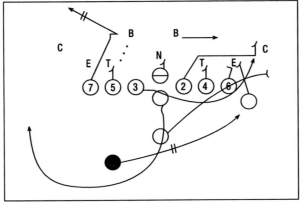

Diagram 9-10

PG   Base, fold
C   Base, away (since the PG is base, the center does not need to seal first).
FB   Kick or log the first man to show outside of the wing's block.

• Left fly 38 sweep vs. the 43 defense (Diagram 9-11)

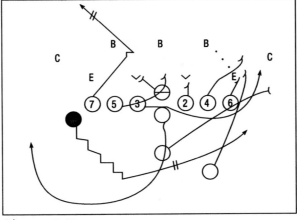

Diagram 9-11

• Right double 38 sweep vs. the split defense (Diagram 9-12)

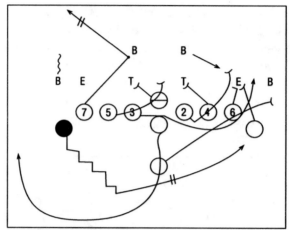

Diagram 9-12

Coaching Point

The playside guard and playside tackle must call a switch if the playside guard cannot base his man.

• Right 38 sweep vs. the eagle defense (Diagram 9-13)

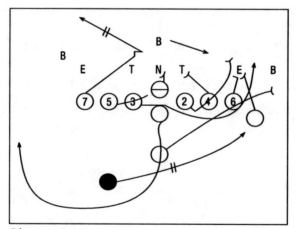

Diagram 9-13

Coaching Point

The playside guard and the playside tackle must call for a switch in assignments if the PG cannot base his man.

The 50 is a combination of the 20 and 30 series. Both the guards and the fullback pull to the sweep. All assignments remain the same as in the 20 series, except for the fullback who escorts through the hole, reading the hat of the playside guard for the cut. In reality, the backside guard and the fullback enter the hole shoulder-to-shoulder.

• Right 58 sweep vs. the 52 defense (Diagram 9-14)

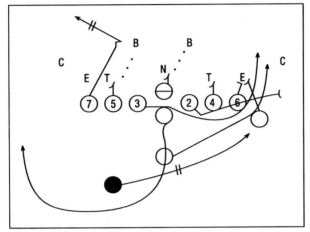

Diagram 9-14

©Mark Faram

The 50 is a combination of the 20 and 30 series.

• Left fly 58 sweep vs. the 43 defense (Diagram 9-15)

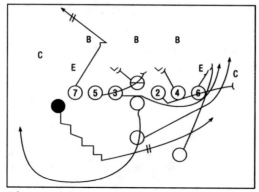

Diagram 9-15

• Right double 58 sweep vs. the split defense (Diagram 9-16)

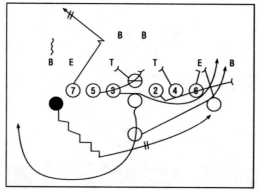

Diagram 9-16

• Right 58 sweep vs. the eagle defense (Diagram 9-17)

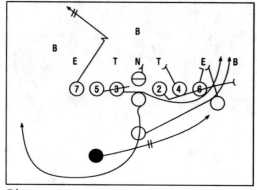

Diagram 9-17

Coaching Point

The fullback carries the ball on the sweeps when a 40 series sweep call is made.

❑ *The 40 Series Sweep Call*

This series sweep call means that the fullback carries the ball on the sweeps. The 40 series assignments on the sweeps are the same as in the 20 series. The backfield break is different.

• Right 48 sweep vs. the 52 defense (Diagram 9-18)

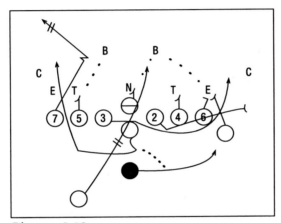

Diagram 9-18

New assignments are:

FB   Get a slight belly path; receive the pitch and cut on the play guard's hat.

HB   Slant through the outside foot of the center; take a fake from the quarterback and sell the trap.

QB   Reverse pivot and pitch the ball to the fullback; turn to the HB slant and sell the trap; then sell the counter carry.

Coaching Point

The 40 series break also carries out the "three points of attack" on each snap.

• Left fly 48 sweep vs. the 43 defense (Diagram 9-19)

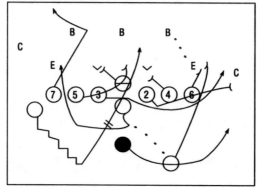

Diagram 9-19

• Right double 48 sweep vs. the split defense (Diagram 9-20)

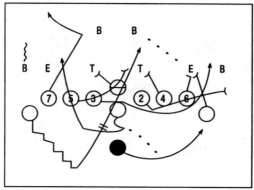

Diagram 9-20

• Right 48 sweep vs. the eagle defense (Diagram 9-21)

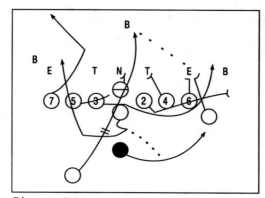

Diagram 9-21

Supplemental Complementary Plays for the 40 Series Sweep

❑ *Play #1: The 42 Tom Trap (Tackle Trap)*

- Right 42 Tom trap vs. 52 defense (Diagram 9-22)

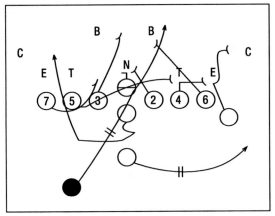

Diagram 9-22

PG	Lead, influence
C	Post, base
PT	Influence downman on, BAB
PE	BAB
BG	Base
BT	Trap the first downman past the center.
BE	Seal the PT hole.
WB	Fake lead and wall contain.
FB	Fake the sweep.
QB	Fake the pitch, turn and give the ball to the HB, and then fake the counter.
HB	Slant at the outside foot of the center, take the ball, and cut on the BAB block.

Coaching Point

On the 42 Tom trap play, the quarterback should fake the pitch, turn and give the ball to the halfback, and then fake the counter.

• Left fly 42 Tom trap vs. the 43 defense (Diagram 9-23)

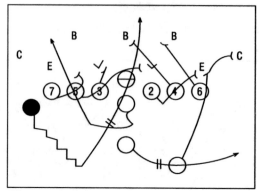

Diagram 9-23

• Right double 42 Tom trap vs. the split defense (Diagram 9-24)

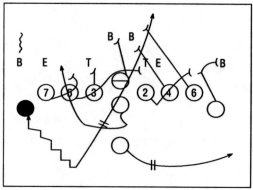

Diagram 9-24

• Right 24 Tom trap vs. the eagle defense (Diagram 9-25)

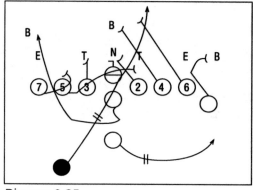

Diagram 9-25

❑ *Play #2: The 47 QB Counter Down*

• Right 47 QB counter down vs. the 52 defense (Diagram 9-26)

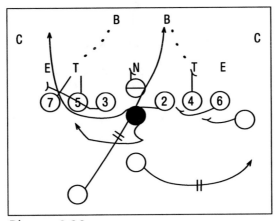

Diagram 9-26

PE	Down, combo
PT	Down, combo
PG	Trap/log the first man outside of the PE's down block.
C	Base, away
BG	Escort
BT	Seal, base
BE	Seal, base
W	Seal, base
FB	Fake the sweep.
HB	Sell the trap.
QB	Fake the pitch, sell the trap, tuck the ball, and read the PG's hat for the cut.

Coaching Point

On the 47 QB counter down play, the quarterback should fake the pitch, sell the trap, tuck the ball, and read the playside guard's hat for the cut.

• Left fly 47 QB counter down vs. the 43 defense (Diagram 9-27)

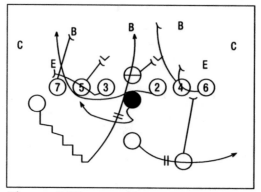

Diagram 9-27

• Right double 47 QB counter down vs. the split defense (Diagram 9-28)

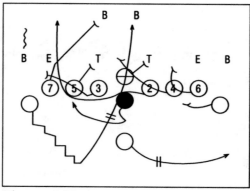

Diagram 9-28

• Right 47 QB counter down vs. the eagle defense (Diagram 9-29)

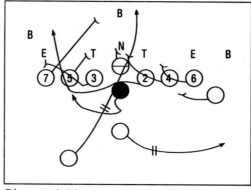

Diagram 9-29

❑ *The Down-Blocking Scheme on Sweep Plays*
  • Right 28 sweep vs. the 52 defense (Diagram 9-30)

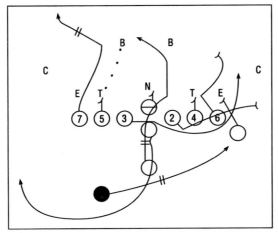

Diagram 9-30

All assignments are the same as in the power-blocking scheme except:

Wing/HB   Down on man on tight end, combo
PE   Down, combo
PT   Down, combo
C   Base, away

On the power-blocking scheme, the center base blocks away.

• Left fly 28 sweep down vs. the 43 defense (Diagram 9-31)

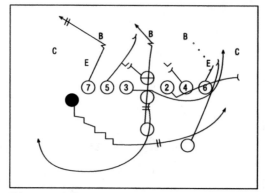

Diagram 9-31

• Right double 28 sweep down vs. the split defense (Diagram 9-32)

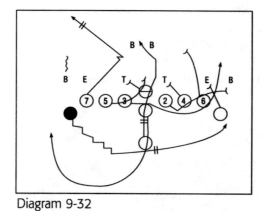

Diagram 9-32

• Right 28 sweep down vs. the eagle defense (Diagram 9-33)

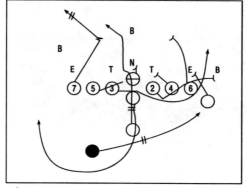

Diagram 9-33

❏ *The Base-Blocking Scheme on Sweep Plays*

The base scheme on sweep plays means that the offense is actually going to attempt to out-distance the defense wide. By stretching the defense, the offense will either be successful in getting wide or will get a cut-up or a cut-back, while the defenders are in a stretched situation.

• Right 28 sweep base vs. the 52 defense (Diagram 9-34)

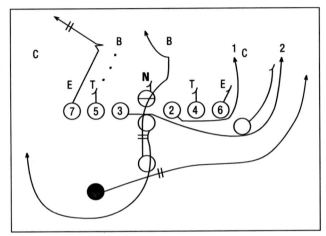

Diagram 9-34

WB/HB	Base-reach block #4 or the contain man.
PE	Base
PT	Base, down
PG	Pull alley #1, which is three yards outside of the PE's block. The PG secures his block first.
C	Seal, base
BG	Pull alley #2, which is three yards outside of wing/halfback's reach block. This block is secured first.
BT	Seal, base.
BE	As usual, when backside from the sweep.

All other backs remain the same in relation to the series called.

Coaching Point

    Stretching the defense enables the offense to be successful either by getting wide or by getting a cut-up or a cut-back, while the defenders are in a stretched situation.

• Left fly 28 sweep base vs. the 43 defense (Diagram 9-35)

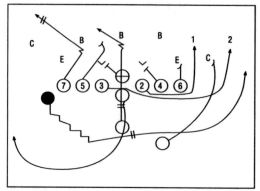

Diagram 9-35

• Right double 28 sweep base vs. the split defense (Diagram 9-36)

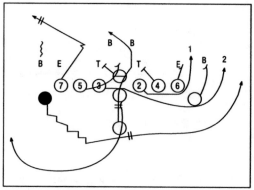

Diagram 9-36

• Right 28 sweep base vs. the eagle defense (Diagram 9-37)

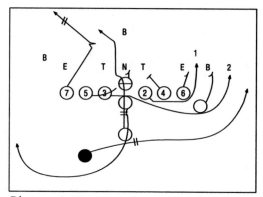

Diagram 9-37

The switch call, when added to the sweep, means that the wing and the tight end to the side of the sweep switch assignments—the wing blocks down and the tight end pulls around and reach blocks the contain man. This "switch" call has proven very effective as a surprise to the defenders. The "switch" is called off the double formation, because the offense gets a "jump" on the defense with the momentum of the fly back. The defense cannot key the fly, since the offense flies and counters and uses the sweep-boot back behind the fly action. The "switch" call is also made from the 50 series.

• Right 58 sweep base switch vs. the 52 defense (Diagram 9-38)

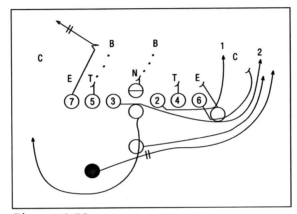

Diagram 9-38

All assignments remain the same as the base call, except for the wing and the tight end.

• Right double 58 sweep base switch vs. the 43 defense (Diagram 9-39)

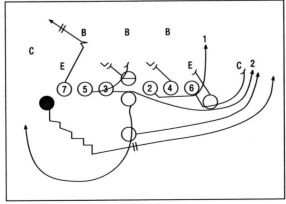

Diagram 9-39

- Right double 58 sweep base switch vs. the split defense (Diagram 9-40)

- Right 58 sweep base switch vs. the eagle defense (Diagram 9-41)

Many 8-man front defenses do not commit their contain man to the line of scrimmage until the keys are read.

Many 8-man front defenses do not commit their contain man to the line of scrimmage until the keys are read.

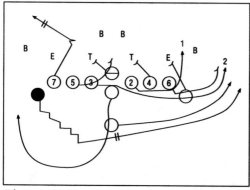

Diagram 9-40

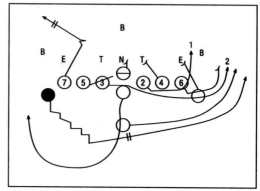

Diagram 9-41

- Right double 58 sweep base switch vs. the 52 defense (Diagram 9-42)

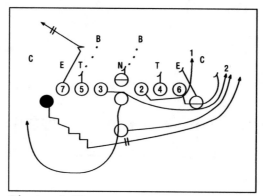

Diagram 9-42

Coaching Point

The "switch" is called off the double formation, because the offense gets a "jump" on the defense with the momentum of the fly back.

❏ *The Toss Sweep*

The offense also runs the "toss sweep," which is being employed in wholesale fashion by many teams across the country, because everyone wants to get the extra blocker in the person of the quarterback. Since the offense already employs the word "toss" in the fullback trap toss to the tight end play, the word "pitch" is added to the sweep plays when the quarterback is asked to lead the play. The word "pitch" is added to any of the sweeps and to all of the series and all of the formations. The double formation with the fly back works well with the pitch. Diagram 9-43 illustrates the pitch sweep out of the left fly formation—a play which is often successful, because the defense usually does not expect a sweep into the tight end-halfback side of the formation.

• Left fly 58 sweep base pitch vs. the 52 defense (Diagram 9-43)

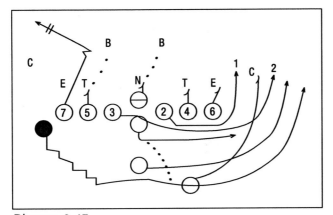

Diagram 9-43

The "toss sweep" is widely employed by many teams across the country.

❏ *The Inside Sweep (26 and 27)*

On occasion, a situation will occur in a game where the defense assumes an alignment, as if to say "you are not going to run the sweep tonight." Even though some of these defenses, by aligning to stop the sweep, loosened and allowed the counter, the mis-direction wing-T with three points of attack provides the offense with the capability to run the inside sweep.

• Right 26 sweep down vs. the 52 defense (Diagram 9-44)

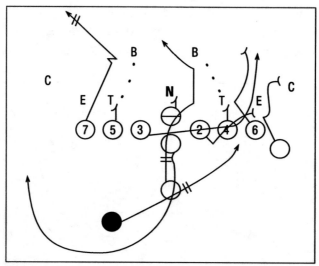

Diagram 9-44

PE	Down, combo, BAB
PT	Down, combo
PG	Trap the first downman past the PT.
C	Base, away
BG	Escort
BT	Seal, base
BE	Usual assignment on sweeps away.
FB	Sell the trap through the linebacker.
Wing	Suba (set up the DE and block away).
HB	Slant through the FB's heels; take the ball, and cut the hole.
QB	Sell the trap; do not force the HB deep; give on the sweep, and sell the boot.

• Left fly 26 sweep down vs. 43 defense (Diagram 9-45)

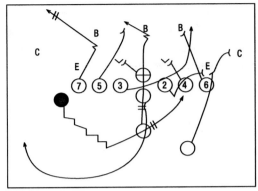

Diagram 9-45

• Right double 26 sweep down vs. the split defense (Diagram 9-46)

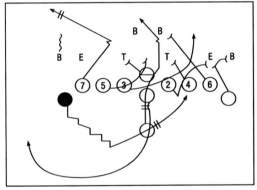

Diagram 9-46

• Right 26 sweep down vs. the eagle defense (Diagram 9-47)

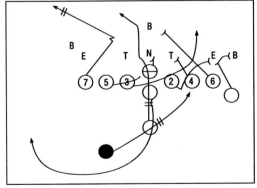

Diagram 9-47

If the fullback is an effective blocker, the inside sweep is mixed on both the 20 and the 30 series. Sometimes, the 30 sweep is more effective, since the first downman on or inside of the play tackle is doubled up, thereby creating a bigger hole. On the other hand, the trap fake, which is really preferred whenever possible, is lost on the play.

  • Right 36 sweep vs. the 52 defense (Diagram 9-48)

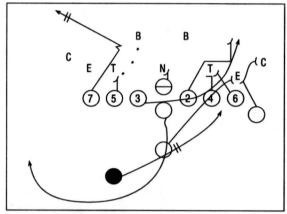

Diagram 9-48

Essentially, all assignments are the same as in the 20 series except:

PG   Base, post
FB   It is very important to get the proper angle to get an inside-out blocking angle and kick out the first downman outside the PT.

  • Left fly 36 sweep vs. the 43 defense (Diagram 9-49)

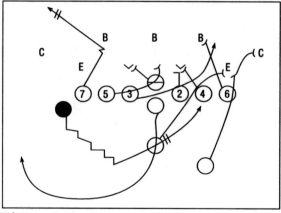

Diagram 9-49

• Right double 36 sweep vs. the split defense (Diagram 9-50)

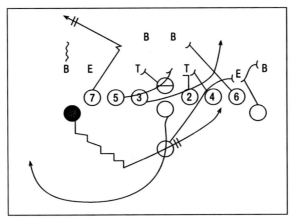

Diagram 9-50

• Right 36 sweep vs. the eagle defense (Diagram 9-51)

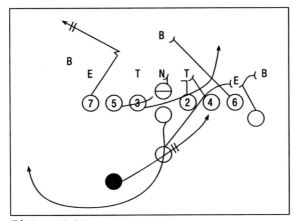

Diagram 9-51

A quarterback counter play off the 20 series inside sweep can be a very effective play. The blocking is the same as for the 47 QB counter from the 40 series, as detailed earlier. It is important that the quarterback stay low, in order to keep from exposing himself too early to the defense.

• Right 17 QB counter down vs. the 52 defense (Diagram 9-52)

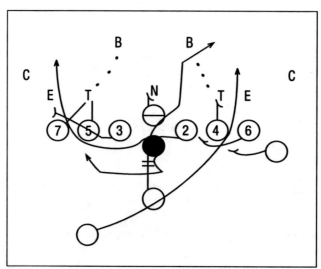

Diagram 9-52

PE	Down, combo
PT	Down, combo
PG	Trap/log first outside of the PE's down.
C	Base, away
BG	Escort
BT	Seal, base
BE	Seal, base
WB/HB	Seal
FB	Sell the trap.
HB	Lift the inside arm when going past the QB; fake the inside sweep.
QB	Sell the trap, step back, and tuck the ball, as the HB comes by. Stay low and read the hat of the trap/log.

• Left fly 17 QB counter down vs. the 43 defense (Diagram 9-53)

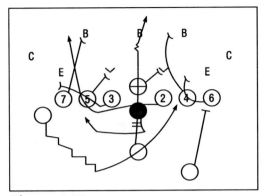

Diagram 9-53

• Right double 17 QB counter down vs. the split defense (Diagram 9-54)

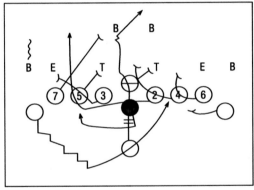

Diagram 9-54

• Right 17 QB counter down vs. the eagle defense (Diagram 9-55)

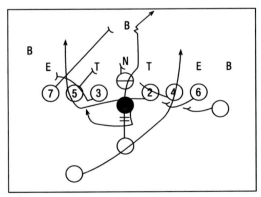

Diagram 9-55

The Sweep Boot Package

The sweep boot package is the third leg of the "three points of attack" off of the sweep break. The fakes by the backs in selling the fullback trap and in selling the sweep, along with the philosophy that the quarterback must come out with "run intent" and attack the defense, are the keys to a successful bootleg package. If the quarterback uses all of his speed from the snap and gets outside of the defense, he has the option of either the run or the pass. Not surprisingly, this aspect really puts pressure on the defense.

More often than not, a very high percentage of the bootleg plays result in big yardage gains or in touchdowns. The bootlegs are also very good calls in short-yardage and goal line situations, if the "run-first intent" is accomplished. Anytime the quarterback gets outside with both the run and the pass options open, very good things can happen.

❑ *The 20 Series Sweep Boot (28 and 29)*
  • Right 28 sweep boot vs. the 52 defense (Diagram 10-1)

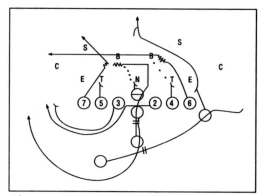

Diagram 10-1

PE	Sell the BAB and break the flag angle.
PT	Base down
PG	Serve as the wall guard. Pull deep (three yards deep from behind the heels of the PTE). Eye in on the first unblocked opponent. Get a wall-in position and prevent him from moving outside.
C	Seal, base, away
BG	Serve as the escort guard. Pull, as in the trap; track the wall guard. Get a depth of four yards from the PTE's heels. Wall in any color coming to the quarterback. Both guards must "spring" the QB outside.
BT	Seal, base, hinge
BE	Sell the BAB, cut across at a basic 10-12 yards deep. Find a "hole" between 6 and 15 yards deep. Hang when open; run when covered.
FB	Sell the trap up to five yards. Plug anyone coming to the quarterback. Slide to the ball side, but do not pass the PTE position. Then, stop and become a safety-valve receiver.
WB	Hit the DE hard, and then get an angle at the middle of the goal posts. Do not cross the original position of the football. Fly deep, but if covered, execute a comeback to 15 yards.
HB	Sell the sweep until reaching the line of scrimmage, and then widen and "die off," while observing the defensive coverage for a throwback call.
QB	Sell the trap and the sweep. Hide the ball from the ball side of the defense. Use all his speed from the snap. Do not "hang;" attack the defense all the way. Get outside of all opponents and take the run. If an open receiver is spotted, throw the ball on the run. If no one is open, take the run. At the point that the QB knows he is running, he should yell "GO" to his guards, so that they may cross the line of scrimmage.

Coaching Points

✓ The guards must not cross the line of scrimmage unless they hear "GO" by the quarterback.

✓ The quarterback may still throw even if he has made the go call, if he notes that the guards have not crossed.

✓ Half of the bootlegs should be called off the fly action. In addition, half of the bootlegs should be made into the short side of the field.

✓ The fakes and the quarterback mechanics are the keys to a successful bootleg attack.

• Left fly 28 sweep boot vs. the 43 defense (Diagram 10-2)

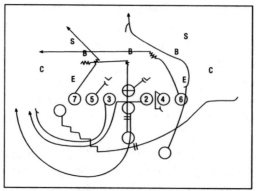

Diagram 10-2

• Right double 28 sweep boot vs. the split defense (Diagram 10-3)

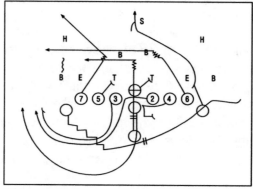

Diagram 10-3

• Right 28 sweep boot vs. the eagle defense (Diagram 10-4)

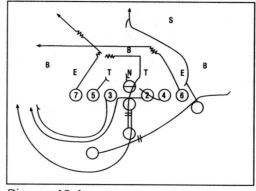

Diagram 10-4

❏ *Change-up Calls for Sweep Boot Patterns*

All assignments remain the same except for the receiver.
- 28 sweep boot "switch" (Diagram 10-5):
  ✓ The tight ends switch assignments from their basic patterns.
  ✓ The PE fakes the BAB and corkscrews into the sideline to daylight depth.
  ✓ The BE fakes the BAB and runs the flag.

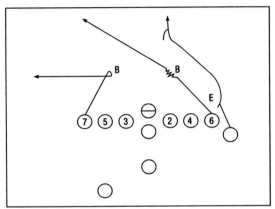

Diagram 10-5

- 28 sweep boot "quick-drag" (Diagram 10-6):
  ✓ The PE releases inside and sprints to the sideline, no deeper than two yards.
  ✓ The BE runs the flag.
  ✓ The wing drags across to daylight.

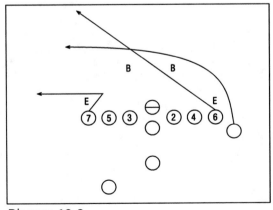

Diagram 10-6

Coaching Points for Sweep Boot-Pattern Strategy:

✓ If the defense is covering the flat with the contain man, then call the basic pattern, as the defensive end and inside linebacker will be assigned to contain the quarterback. In this case, the guards should be able to propel the quarterback outside in a run situation. As a result, the contain man is placed in a "hot box;" he has to either drop the receiver or allow the run.

✓ If the defense is bringing the contain man to the quarterback, the "quick-drag" pattern should be called. In this instance, the PE will "out run" the coverage of the inside linebacker and become open. If the linebacker is fortunate to be able to cover the PE to the sideline, then the drag man has an excellent chance to spring open.

©Mark Faram

If the linebacker is able to cover the playside end to the sideline when a sweep boot pattern is called, the drag man has an excellent chance to spring open.

• The 28 sweep boot "throwback" (Diagram 10-7)

If the defense does not assign someone to cover the sweep back, then get on the "throwback" right now.

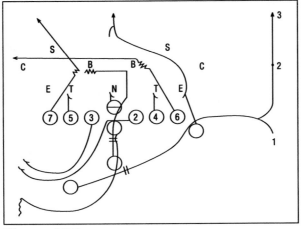

Diagram 10-7

All assignments remain the same as in counter lateral except:

✓ *The guards* will build a passing "pocket" three yards outside of the tight end.
✓ *The quarterback* will set up in the pocket and drop off pumping to the receivers as he checks the throwback area.
✓ *The halfback* will run the sweep to the line of scrimmage. Then, he will sprint out to the sideline to a point 10 yards wide and run the pattern as called:

1 call—face the quarterback on the line.
2 call—turn upfield and hang between 7 and 10 yards.
3 call—fly deep.

Coaching Point

On the 28 sweep boot "throwback" play, if the defense does not assign someone to cover the sweep back, the quarterback should get on the "throwback" right now.

Coaching Point

> The 28 sweep GOB play is very important to the offense, since it is a "key break" to the defense.

• 28 sweep GOB (Diagram 10-8)

GOB means that the guards pull opposite the ball. This play involves a naked bootleg. On this play, the entire team executes the sweep play, but no one crosses the line of scrimmage to block. The naked boot could result in a pass. The quarterback must sell the trap, sell the sweep, and hide the ball. He must come out with run-first intent. The backside tight end runs a flag pattern, as he does on all sweeps away from his side. The success of this play depends entirely upon the skill of the quarterback. This play is very important to the offense, since it is a "key break" to the defense.

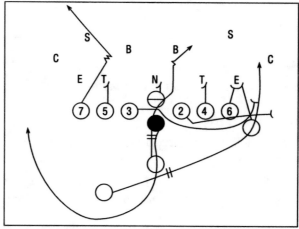

Diagram 10-8

• The sweep keep (28 and 29)

When "boot" is called, the ball will be going away from the flow of the play. The word "keep" means that the ball will be kept to the flow of the play. Both boots and keeps are run/pass plays with "run-intent" first. The keep play is very important to the offense, since the offense must show the defense that it will throw the ball with the flow of the play. The sweep keep is liberally mixed with the sweep boot.

Coaching Point

> The keep play is very important to the offense, since the offense must show the defense that it will throw the ball with the flow of the play.

• Right 28 sweep keep vs. the 52 defense (Diagram 10-9)

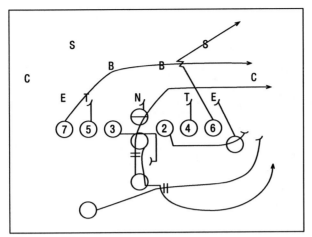

Diagram 10-9

PE   Fake BAB and flag.
PT   Base, down
PG   Pull and check alley 1, then alley 2. Do not cross the line of scrimmage unless the quarterback yells "GO." The PG must block base if he and the PT are both covered by downmen.
C   Base, away
BG   Pull and check the 2 hole. If no one comes through the 2 hole, then hinge back for the chase man. If the PG and the center are both covered by downmen, the PG must block base.
BT   Base, in gap, hinge
BE   Fake BAB and cross at 15 yards deep.
WB   Block down on the defensive end.
FB   Sell the trap and then get into the flat at three yards deep.
HB   Sell the sweep as long as possible, then lock-up block on the first color to show.
QB   Sell the trap; sell the sweep. Get a short ride on the sweep back, then come off with "run first intent," looking for an open receiver. The QB should yell "GO" if he decides to run.

Coaching Point

On the 28 sweep keep play, the halfback should sell the sweep as long as possible and then execute a lock-up block on the first color to show.

• Left fly 28 sweep keep vs. the 43 defense (Diagram 10-10)

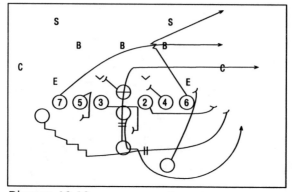

Diagram 10-10

• Right double 28 sweep keep vs. the split defense (Diagram 10-11)

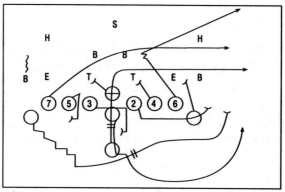

Diagram 10-11

• Right 28 sweep keep vs. the eagle defense (Diagram 10-12)

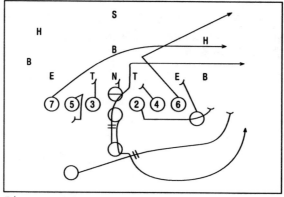

Diagram 10-12

The Option Package

I firmly believe that all offensive systems should be able to run some type of an option in order to force the defense to align to stop it. Since the option is not basic to our offensive scheme, we try to keep it as simple as possible for our players. The option is a part of our 40 series, because the fullback's path differs from the 20, 30, and 50 series.

❏ *The 44 Slant (45 to the Left)*
  • Right 44 slant vs. the 52 defense (Diagram 11-1)

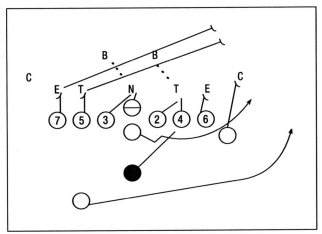

Diagram 11-1

Coaching Point

   Against 7-man front defenses, the zone block is preferred, although the offense can totally base it.

• Left fly 44 slant vs. the 43 defense (Diagram 11-2)

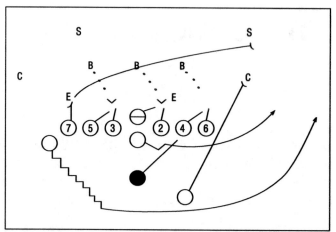

Diagram 11-2

Against 7-man front defenses, the "zone block" is preferred, although the ofense can totally base it.

FB	Slant through the butt of the PT, receive the ball, cover it with both forearms, and run to daylight.
QB	Get the ball to the fullback as soon as possible, and as deep as possible. Get a slight ride, then come out from behind the fullback and attack the end with speed.
HB	Maintain the pitch relationship to the quarterback. The HB must hurry.
WB	Base

Coaching Point

   On the left fly 44 slant vs. the 43 defense, the fullback should slant through the butt of the playside tackle, get the ball, cover it with both forearms, and run to daylight.

• Right double 44 slant vs. the split defense (Diagram 11-3)

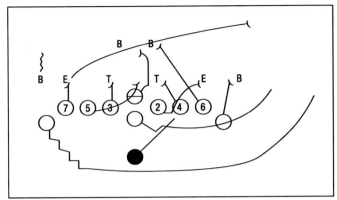

Diagram 11-3

• Right 44 slant vs. the eagle defense (Diagram 11-4)

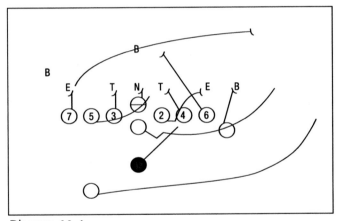

Diagram 11-4

Against 8-man front defenses, which leave the PT uncovered, the G-block is preferred, even though the offense can base it with a fold between the PG and PT. Diagrams 11-3 and 11-4 illustrate the G-block vs. the split and the eagle defenses.

PE   Down
PT   Down
PG   Trap the defensive end.
C   Base, play gap, linebacker
BG   Base
BT   Seal, BAH (block across the hole).
BE   BAH

❑ *The 44 Slant-Option (45 Slant-Option to the Left)*

Simplicity is continued in the option game by zone blocking the option as far as feasible.

• Right 44 slant-option vs. the 52 defense (Diagram 11-5)

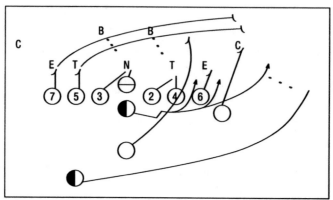

Diagram 11-5

FB   Sell the 44 slant, but become a blocker for the quarterback by finding the linebacker or other unblocked opponent and drive through with the inside shoulder.

QB   Meet the fullback as in the 44 slant, but observe the defensive reaction as he "rides." The QB's first intent should be to keep the ball. Find a hole:
   ✓   Follow the fullback.
   ✓   Cut outside the defensive end.
   ✓   Keep wide.
   ✓   Pitch the ball as a last choice.

• Left fly 44 slant-option vs. the 43 defense (Diagram 11-6)

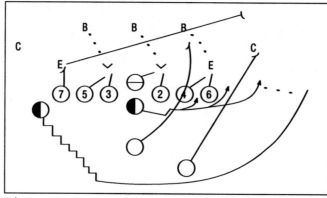

Diagram 11-6

• Right double 44 slant-option vs. the split defense (Diagram 11-7)

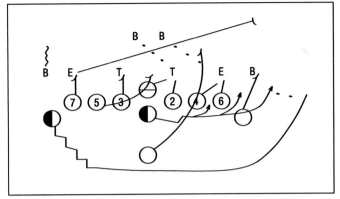

Diagram 11-7

• Right 44 slant-option vs. the eagle defense (Diagram 11-8)

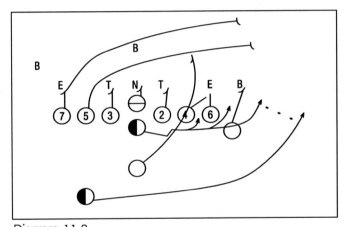

Diagram 11-8

PART III:
SUPPLEMENTAL ACTIVITIES

©Elsburgh Clarke Photography

12

Wing-T Supplement

Over the years, we have supplemented the Wing-T offense with various activities. While some of these supplements have proven to be somewhat unsuccessful, a few have had a positive impact. This chapter presents a discussion of the three supplements that have proven valuable over the years:

- The double wing (without a pre-fly by a wing and snap the ball on first sound)
- The power formation
- The Wing-I formation

The Double Call

To reiterate, when we call "Right Double," both halfbacks will align in the wing positions. The word, "right," called before the "double," means that the left wing will fly. As a result, we are in wing right formation at the snap. The same is true for the "Left Double" call.

Early on, in the more than two decades that my teams employed this offense, I recognized the need to design something from the double formation that did not use the fly action before the snap. The purpose of the no-fly-double wing is to surprise the defense, thereby causing the defenders to first align to cover the double wing in case there is no fly, and, subsequently, to adjust if there was a pre-fly.

The double wing set did not appear to influence the 4-back (7-man front) defenses very much, except to cause the cornerbacks or contain men to align deeper until the fly occurred (Diagrams 12-1 and 12-2).

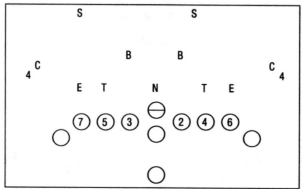

Diagram 12-1

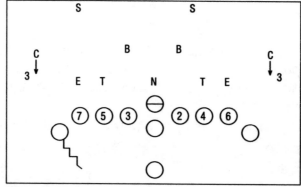

Diagram 12-2

The double wing set did influence the alignment of the 3-back (8-man front) defenses to some extent, by causing the outside linebackers to align much deeper until a pre-fly occurred. When the wing left on the pre-fly, the contain linebacker had to move to the contain position very quickly and rarely made it to the line of scrimmage before the snap. It should be remembered that the fly we use is a full speed one-count movement (Diagram 12-3).

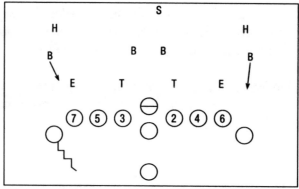

Diagram 12-3

In the double wing (no fly) formation, a "suddenly dropback pass" attack was implemented to try to take advantage of the defense.

- "Suddenly dropback pass" vs. the 4-back, 7-man front type of defense

We have found that the vast majority of these 4-back defenses will employ cover 2 (halves) style of pass and contain coverage. The cornerbacks will align four yards deep and four yards wide, while the safeties will align 10-12 yards deep and head up on the tight ends (Diagram 12-4).

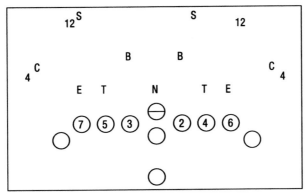

Diagram 12-4

If the tight ends release, the safeties will cover their half of the field, while the corners will cover the flats. If the tight ends block, the corners will contain and the safeties will support. With these facts in mind, we designed our "suddenly dropback pass" patterns.

Coaching Point

Our "suddenly dropback pass" patterns are based on the fact that if the tight ends release, the safeties will cover their half of the field, while the corners will cover the flats; and if the tight ends block, the corners will contain, and the safeties will support.

• Double dropback call vs. the 4-back cover 2 (Diagrams 12-5 and 12-6)

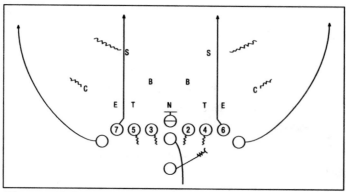

Diagram 12-5

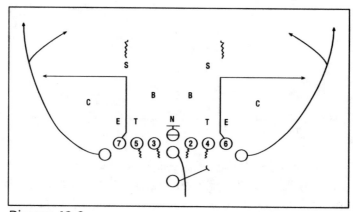

Diagram 12-6

Tight Ends Get upfield via the best release. Run at the safety. If the safety leaves, continue deep and look for the ball inside. If the safety stays, square out and sprint to the sideline looking for the ball.

Wings Come off at full speed. Get depth and width. Force the defense to cover the entire field. Outrun the corner coverage. If the corner does not cover him deep, the wings should look for the "fly ball" inside. If the corner mans the wing, the wing should outrun him, while looking for the fly ball. If the corner does a good job in manning the wings, the wings should cut to the post.

Quarterback Open to the QB's right, drop seven steps, as he keys the safety's action and surveys the field. The scout report of each opponent will identify suspect personnel.

Coaching Point

If the defensive scheme involves an alignment in which there is a single safety, the tight ends release wide outside and sprint deep, looking inside for the ball.

- Double dropback call vs. 3-back zone coverage (Diagram 12-7)

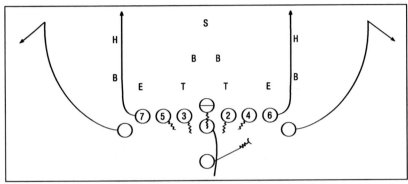

Diagram 12-7

When a single safety alignment is observed:

Tight Ends	Release wide outside (stretch the middle zone). Sprint deep, looking inside for the ball.
Wings	Basic wide-deep release. The wings will draw corner coverage either man or zone. The wings should entertain the cornerback by making the corner stretch to them and then execute a sideline comeback. If the wings get the outside linebacker on man-to-man coverage, they should beat him deep.
Quarterback	Same as described for 4-back coverage.

Coaching Point

If outside linebacker coverage on the wings is drawn, we will add "B Swing" to the call (B is the fullback), as shown in Diagram 12-8.

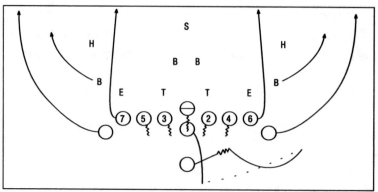

Diagram 12-8

- Pass protection for the double dropback call
  - ✓ vs. 52 (Diagram 12-9)

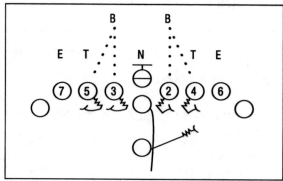

Diagram 12-9

  - ✓ vs. 43 (Diagram 12-10)

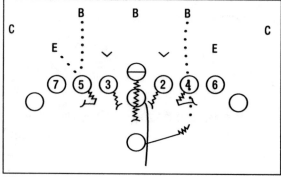

Diagram 12-10

✓ vs. split (Diagram 12-11)

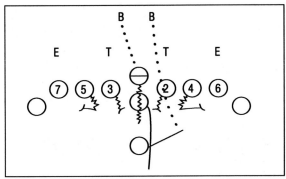

Diagram 12-11

✓ vs. the eagle (Diagram 12-12)

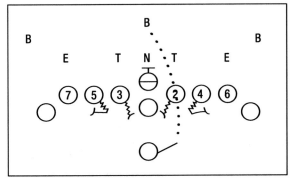

Diagram 12-12

Bear in mind that this action is a sudden surprise for the defense which must purely react to the play without focus time. Accordingly, we snap the ball on the first sound.

The front 5 will drop back quickly at the snap, reading the man coming to their zone. This situation involves a "cup-number" scheme.

C   zero zone.
G's 1 zone.
T's 2 zone.
FB block #3 to right.

Coaching Point

If the defense comes with seven rushers, the weakside defensive end would be free. The problem for the defense is that they have to predict when this play will come.

❑ *The Power Set (a Supplement to the Wing-T)*

In this set, the halfback aligns over to the side of the wing. All other positions remain the same. Our huddle call is "power right" and "power left" (Diagrams 12-13 and 12-14).

• Power right (Diagram 12-13)

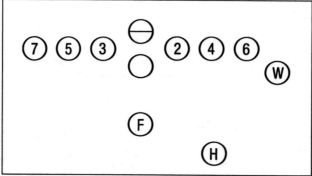

Diagram 12-13

• Power left (Diagram 12-14)

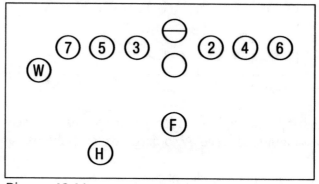

Diagram 12-14

The majority of the basic offense can be run from the power set.
- The fullback package (Chapter 6)
- The counter package (Chapter 7)
- The counter-boot package (Chapter 8)
- The 40 sweep to the power side
- The 20, 30 and 50 sweeps to the weak side
- The sweep-boot package (showing weak sweep and booting back to power)
- The option package (Chapter 11)

• The counter break (Diagram 12-15)

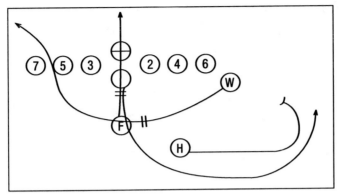

Diagram 12-15

• Sweep break—20 series strong (Diagram 12-16)

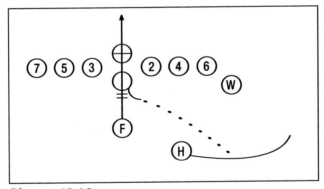

Diagram 12-16

• Sweep break—40 series (Diagram 12-17)

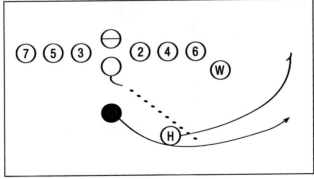

Diagram 12-17

• Sweep break—20 series weak (Diagram 12-18)

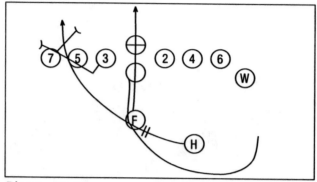

Diagram 12-18

• Sweep break—30 and 50 series weak (Diagram 12-19)

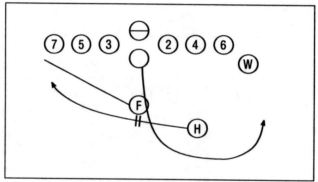

Diagram 12-19

The majority of the Misdirection Wing-T offense can be run from a power set.

❑ *The Strongside Shoot Call (28 and 29 Shoot)*

The play that gets advantage on the defense (if the defenders fail to adjust) is the shoot call to the strong or wing side. We will call this play early in our game plan from the power set. This step forces the defense to adjust to stop this play. We will then go to whatever the adjustment gives us—particularly, the weakside.

• Power right 28 shoot down vs. the 52 defense (Diagram 12-20)

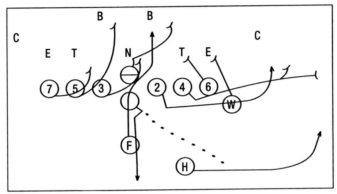

Diagram 12-20

• Power right 28 shoot base vs. the 43 defense (Diagram 12-21)

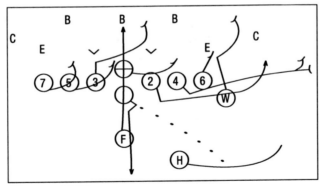

Diagram 12-21

Coaching Point

Note the base call.

• Power right 28 shoot base vs. the split defense (Diagram 12-22)

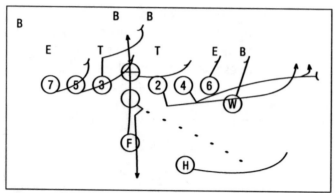

Diagram 12-22

Coaching Point

Note the base call.

• Power right 28 shoot vs. the eagle defense (Diagram 12-23)

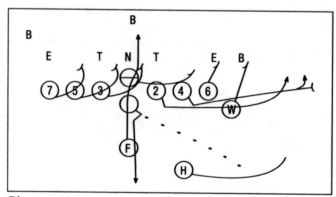

Diagram 12-23

Coaching Point

Note the base call.

❑ *The Wing-I Set (as a Supplement to the Wing-T)*

The halfback will align over to the wing side in the tailback position. All other positions will remain the same. The huddle call is, "I Right" and "I Left" (Diagrams 12-24 and 12-25).

• I right (Diagram 12-24)

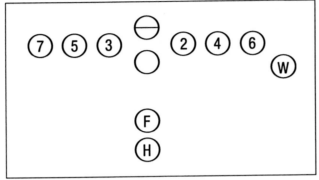

Diagram 12-24

• I left (Diagram 12-25)

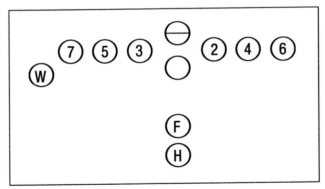

Diagram 12-25

The majority of the basic offense can be run from the I set:
• The fullback package (Chapter 6)
• The counter package (Chapter 7)
• The counter boot package (Chapter 8)
• The 20, 30, and 50 sweep package (Chapter 9)
• The option package (Chapter 11)

  • Counter break (Diagram 12-26)

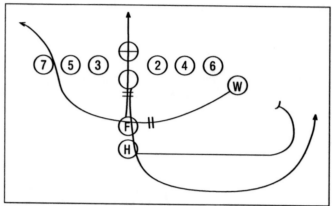

Diagram 12-26

  • Sweep break—20 series (Diagram 12-27)

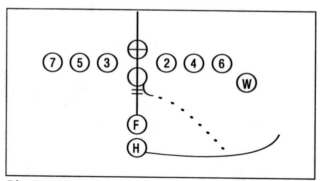

Diagram 12-27

  • Sweep break—30,50 series (Diagram 12-28)

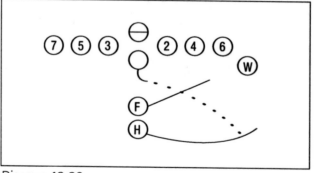

Diagram 12-28

The play that we like to call out of the Wing-I formation is the 50 sweep. This play jumps on the defense "in a hurry." After we see what defensive adjustments are made, other plays from the Wing-I are mixed.

• I right 58 sweep base vs. the 52 defense (Diagram 12-29)

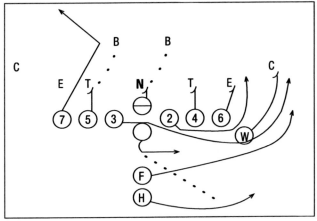

Diagram 12-29

• I right 58 sweep base switch (Diagram 12-30)
   ✓ We also like to add the "switch" call off the base scheme.

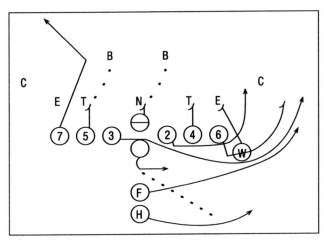

Diagram 12-30

Coaching Point

As was previously discussed, the "switch" call tells the wing to block down and the tight end to pull and base.

• I right 58 sweep base vs. the 43 defense (Diagram 12-31)

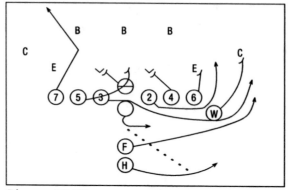

Diagram 12-31

• I right 58 sweep base vs. the split defense (Diagram 12-32)

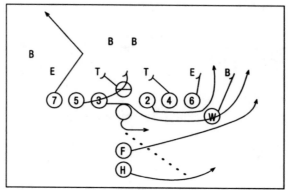

Diagram 12-32

• I right 58 sweep base vs. the eagle defense (Diagram 12-33)

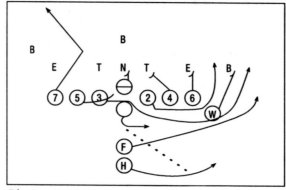

Diagram 12-33

13

The Split-End Side Attack

The Delaware wing-T was developed in the early 1950s and quickly became one of the leading offenses in the country. Although additional offensive systems have experienced popularity over the years (e.g., the spread offense), the wing-T continues to be widely accepted after more than five decades.

In the early years of the wing-T, all teams employed double tight ends. As defenses began to "catch up" with the offense, however, coaches started splitting the end away from the wingside. The split of the backside end caused defenses to adjust to new alignments. As a consequence, the Delaware wing-T experienced a resurgence in popularity.

This chapter details the split-end side attack of the mis-direction wing-T offense. It is important to note that even teams that do not employ the wing-T style of offense, but employ a set where the end is split and the runningback is behind the tackle or nearby, can find value in the suggested plays to the split-end side.

This chapter details the plays to the left only. Coaches who decide to have their teams execute the mis-direction wing-T should flip these nine plays to the right. The plays to the wingside can be found in previous chapters.

❑ *The Play List:*
- X left 29 shoot
- X left 22 trap toss
- X left shoot 23 trap
- X left 19 option
- X left 49 sweep
- X left, right fly 39 sweep
- X left, right fly 36 counter GT down
- X left, right fly 36 counter boot
- X left 25 counter down

❏ *The Formation*

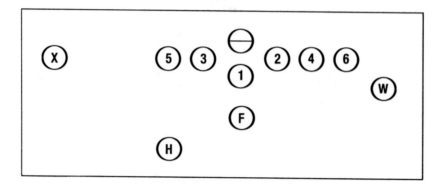

⊖	=	center
2 and 3	=	guards
4 and 5	=	tackles
6	=	TE
X	=	split end (his split will vary from 8-to-15 yards)
W	=	wing
F	=	fullback
H	=	halfback
1	=	quarterback

All other key factors involving the split-end set, such as splits, depths, etc., are specified in previous chapters.

❏ *Blocking Rule Position Symbols*

X	=	split end
PT	=	playside tackle
PG	=	playside guard
C	=	center
BG	=	backside guard
BT	=	backside tackle
BE	=	backside tight end
W	=	wingback
FB	=	fullback
H	=	halfback
QB	=	quarterback
CP	=	coaching point

❑ *X Left 29 Shoot*

X left 29 shoot blocking rules:

X   = Split 12 yards; come down the line under control until the first opponent is located coming to the pitch; wall-block him in.

PT = Pull wide through the original alignment of X; escort the ballcarrier.

PG = Hook the man on the tackle.

C   = Hook the man on the guard.

BG = Hook the man on the center.

BT = Hook the man on the guard.

BE = Hook the man on the tackle.

W   = Hook the man on the end.

F   = Chase the play in case of a fumble.

H   = Sprint flat full-speed; take the pitch and run wide. This is a distance pitch.

QB = run at the halfback as you prepare the pitch; lead him with a spiral pitch; keep your shoulders down; do not "shoot from the hip." This is a distance pitch.

CP = This play is very effective when properly executed with speed. The PT must have decent speed. Note: One of our halfbacks set our school's all-time record of scoring seven touchdowns in one game on this play.

• X left 29 shoot vs. the 52 defense (Diagram 13-1)

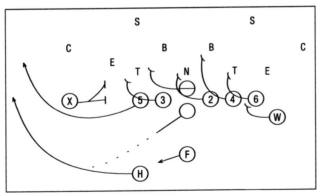

Diagram 13-1

Coaching Points

The keys to this play's success are:

1. The H back must sprint full speed flat toward the sideline, trying to "out-run" the pitch.

2. This forces the quarterback to hustle and make the long distance pitch accurately.

• X left 29 shoot vs. the 43 defense (Diagram 13-2)

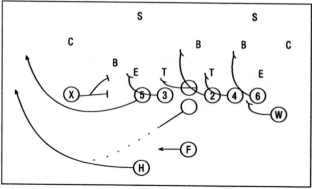

Diagram 13-2

• X left 29 shoot vs. the 44 defense (Diagram 13-3)

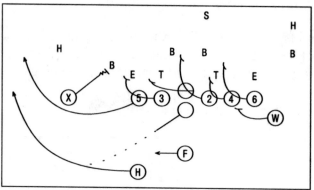

Diagram 13-3

• X left 29 shoot vs. the eagle defense (Diagram 13-4)

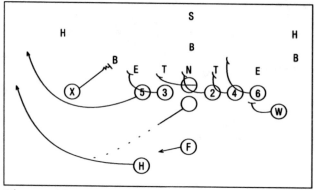

Diagram 13-4

❑ X Left 22 Trap Toss

X left 22 trap toss blocking rules:

X   = Split 12 yards; step up on the outside foot, then break for the middle of the split at five yards deep, looking for the ball. If there is no ball, then plant and flag.

PT = Base

PG = 22 trap

C   = 22 trap down

BG = 22 trap down

BT = Base

BE = Drag across at eight yards deep.

W   = Position and pass block the end.

F   = Take a big step with the right foot and raise the right arm to take the fake; then, break out and set to block the first rusher.

H   = Swing the line of scrimmage at a point just outside of the X position; look for the ball. If there's no ball, then widen as you run upfield.

QB = Pivot, as in 22 trap; quickly show the ball at the fullback; then, turn and quickly throw to the X. If X is covered, drop and check the HB swing. If the swing is covered, drop and check flag, across, and HB wide.

CP = Read the defender in the flat. This defender must choose who he will cover—the X or the swing.

CP = Interior line does not cross the LOS.

• X left 22 trap toss vs. the 52 defense (Diagram 13-5)

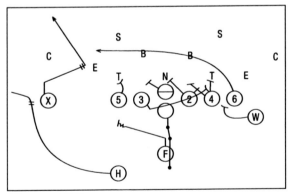

Diagram 13-5

• X left 22 trap toss vs. the 43 defense (diagram 13-6)

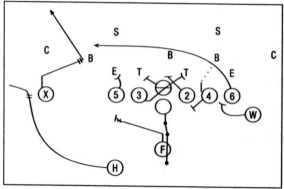

Diagram 13-6

• X left trap toss vs. the 44 defense (Diagram 13-7)

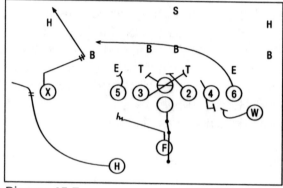

Diagram 13-7

• X left trap toss vs. the eagle defense (Diagram 13-8)

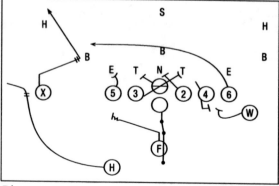

Diagram 13-8

❏ *X Left Shoot 23 Trap Down*

X left shoot 23 trap blocking rules:

X	=	Block the linebacker across the hole.
PT	=	BAB
PG	=	Lead, BAB, SUBA
C	=	Away, post
BG	=	Trap the first down man past the center.
BT	=	Base the linebacker.
BE	=	BAH (block across the hole).
W	=	Release inside the end and cut off the safety.
F	=	Dive, receive the ball, cover the ball, and cut behind the trapper. Get around BAB and upfield. Be so quick through the hole that the trapper must hurry.
H	=	Fake the shoot fully and fast.
QB	=	Quick pivot; hand-off to the FB, continue, and fake the pitch to the HB.

• X left shoot 23 trap down vs. the 52 defense (Diagram 13-9)

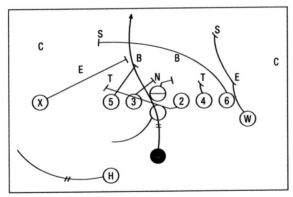

Diagram 13-9

Coaching Point

On the X left shoot 23 trap down play, the quarterback should execute a quick pivot, hand the ball off to the fullback, continue down the line, and then fake the pitch to the halfback.

• X left 23 trap down vs. the 43 defense (Diagram 13-10)

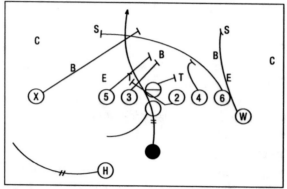

Diagram 13-10

• X left shoot 23 trap down vs. the 44 defense (Diagram 13-11)

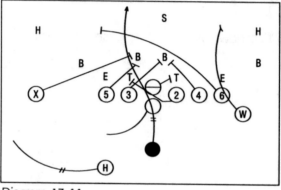

Diagram 13-11

• X left shoot 23 trap down vs. the eagle defense (Diagram 13-12)

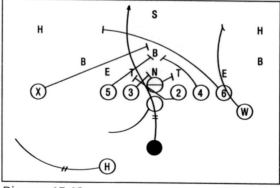

Diagram 13-12

❏ *X Left 19 Option*

X left 19 option blocking rules:

X = Split 10 yards; come down the line, locate the man taking the pitch, position and wall him in.

PT = Base

PG = Base

C = Base

BG = Base; note the two MLBs.

BT = Base; note the two MLBs.

BE = Slam on; BAH.

W = BAH

F = Sprint for width, get some depth, take the pitch, and follow the escort.

H = Escort the pitch and block the first man to come to the pitch man.

QB = Step back, take a slight upward path to attack, and consume the man who is taking you. Break feet and pitch safely. Turn upfield if no one takes you.

• X left 19 option vs. the 52 defense (Diagram 13-13)

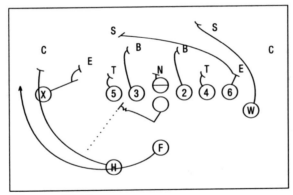

Diagram 13-13

Coaching Point

    On the X left 19 option play, the fullback should sprint for width, get some depth, take the pitch, and then follow the escort.

• X left 19 option vs. the 43 defense (Diagram 13-14)

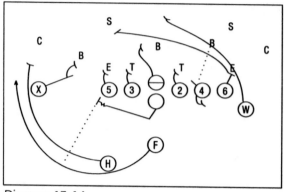

Diagram 13-14

• X left 19 option vs. the 44 defense (Diagram 13-15)

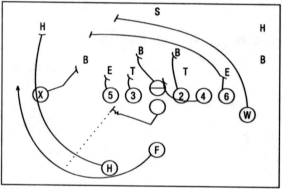

Diagram 13-15

• X left 19 option vs. the eagle defense (Diagram 13-16)

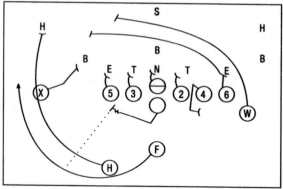

Diagram 13-16

❑ *X Left 49 Sweep*

X left 49 sweep blocking rules:

X	=	Block down on the first threat to the sweep.
PT	=	Base
PG	=	Pull and kick out the contain.
C	=	Seal; base
BG	=	Pull and escort (the escort rule is to block the first man who can tackle the ballcarrier).
BT	=	Seal, base
BE	=	Slam; base; BAH
W	=	BAH
F	=	Take the pitch; carry wide. Cut on the PG's hat.
H	=	Block the end man on the line.
QB	=	Reverse pivot, pitch to the FB, and then escort and look to pick up penetration.
CP	=	If the defense gets penetration through the guard hole, call the 20 sweep, and the PT will block down.

• X left 49 sweep vs. the 52 defense (Diagram 13-17)

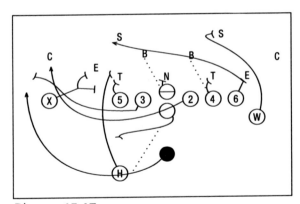

Diagram 13-17

Coaching Point

On the X left 49 sweep play, the quarterback should reverse pivot, pitch to the fullback, and serve as his escort, looking to pick up penetration.

• X left 49 sweep vs. the 43 defense (Diagram 13-18)

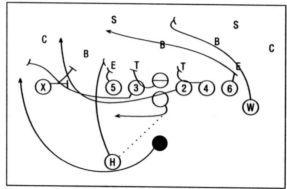

Diagram 13-18

• X left 49 sweep vs. the 44 defense (Diagram 13-19)

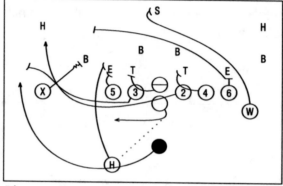

Diagram 13-19

• X left 49 sweep vs. the eagle defense (Diagram 13-20)

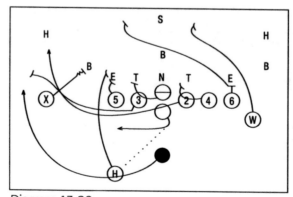

Diagram 13-20

❏ *X Left, Right Fly 39 Sweep*

X left, right fly 39 sweep blocking rules:

    X   = Block down on the first man to show the sweep.
    PT = Base
    PG = Base (30 sweep)
    C   = Base, away
    BG = Escort the sweep.
    BT = Seal; if needed, base.
    BE = Slam; base; BAH.
    W   = Fly and carry the ball; cut on the FB's kick block; follow the escort guard.
    F   = Kick or reach the contain man.
    H   = Block the end man on the line.
    QB = Give the ball to the fly back; then fake the bootleg.
    CP = Also 29 sweep; 59 sweep; sweep boot.

• X left, right fly 39 sweep vs. the 52 defense (Diagram 13-21)

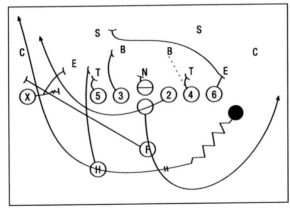

Diagram 13-21

Coaching Point

    On the X left, right fly sweep play, the quarterback should give the ball to the wing (the fly back) and then fake the bootleg.

• X left, right fly 39 sweep vs. the 43 defense (Diagram 13-22)

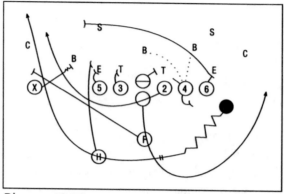

Diagram 13-22

• X left, right fly 39 sweep vs. the 44 defense (Diagram 13-23)

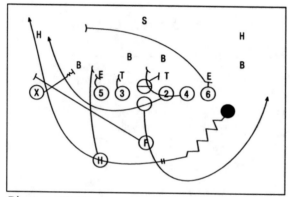

Diagram 13-23

• X left, right fly 39 sweep vs. the eagle defense (Diagram 13-24)

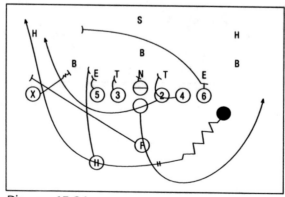

Diagram 13-24

❑ *X Left, Right Fly 36 Counter GT Down*

X left, right fly 36 counter GT down blocking rules:

X	=	Fake a pass pattern route.
BT	=	Escort through the 6 hole.
BG	=	Trap the 6 hole.
C	=	Away
PG	=	Down (color call—switch with the PT).
PT	=	Down (color call—switch with the PG).
BE	=	Down
W	=	Fly and position for the wall block on the DE.
F	=	Plug the first unblocked opponent to come across the line.
H	=	Carry the ball through the 6 counter hole.
QB	=	Give the ball to the counter back and fake the counter boot.
CP	=	GT means guard trap and tackle escort. Down means down-block system. Both factors are previously covered in the book.

• X left, right fly 36 counter GT down vs. the 52 defense (Diagram 13-25)

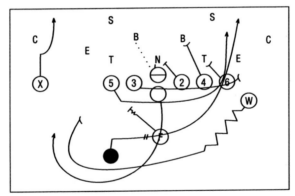

Diagram 13-25

Coaching Point

On the X left, right fly 36 counter GT down play, the halfback carries the ball through the 6 counter hole.

• X left, right fly 36 counter GT down vs. the 43 defense (Diagram 13-26)

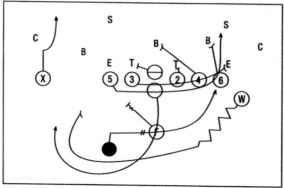

Diagram 13-26

• X left, right fly 36 counter GT down vs. the 44 defense (Diagram 13-27)

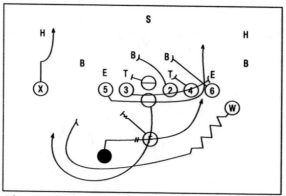

Diagram 13-27

• X left, right fly 36 counter GT down vs. the eagle defense (Diagram 13-28)

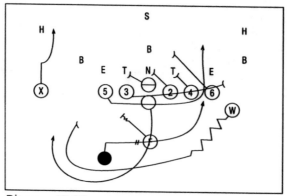

Diagram 13-28

❏ *X Left, Right Fly 36 Counter Boot*

X left, right fly 36 counter boot blocking rules:

X = Slant to the middle of the split; then flag.
PT = Base down if the man is on guard.
PG = Trap the opposite guard hole.
C = Base; seal to the ball; check the linebacker.
BG = Trap the end.
BT = Base (in gap, on, outside); check the linebacker.
BE = Release across the field to a depth of 10-12 yards in the flat.
W = Fly and get a wall-block position on the first man to show.
F = Get in the flat three yards deep.
H = Super fake the 36 counter through the 6 hole; then, check the throwback area. If you're open, inform the coaches.
QB = Sell the counter; then, boot wide and attack the line of scrimmage, as you read run or pass. If the receivers are covered, then run. If there is an "open" receiver, throw to him.

• X left, right fly 39 counter boot vs. the 52 defense (Diagram 13-29)

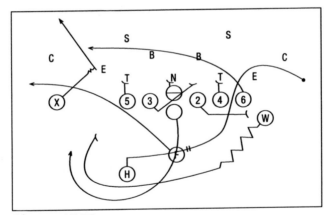

Diagram 13-29

Coaching Point

On the X left, right fly 36 counter boot play, the quarterback should sell the counter, and then boot wide and attack the line of scrimmage, as he reads run or pass. If his receivers are covered, he should run. If there is an open receiver, he should throw to him.

• X left, right fly 39 counter boot vs. the 43 defense (Diagram 13-30)

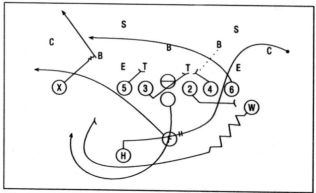

Diagram 13-30

• X left, right fly 36 counter boot vs. the 44 defense (Diagram 13-31)

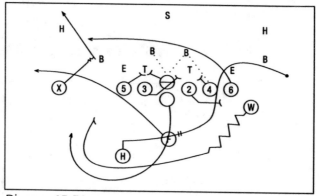

Diagram 13-31

• X left, right fly 36 counter boot vs. the eagle defense (Diagram 13-32)

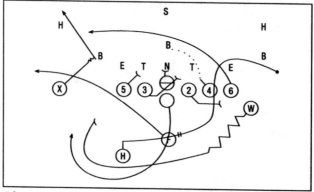

Diagram 13-32

❑ *X Left 25 Counter GT Down*

X left 25 counter GT down blocking rules:

X	=	Split eight yards and BAH (block across the hole).
PT	=	Down (color)
PG	=	Down (color)
C	=	Block away
BG	=	Trap the 5 hole.
BT	=	Escort through the 5 hole.
BE	=	Seal the man on the tackle. If no man is on the tackle, then base block.
W	=	Carry the ball at the 5 hole.
F	=	Super fake the 22 trap play.
H	=	Get a wall position for the boot call.
QB	=	fake the 22 trap play to the fullback, give the ball to the wing, and fake the counter boot.
CP	=	"GT" and "color" are explained in previous chapters.

• X left 25 counter GT down vs. the 52 defense (Diagram 13-33)

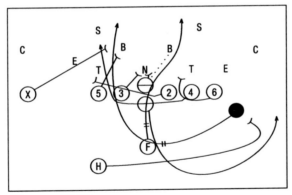

Diagram 13-33

Coaching Point

   On the X left 25 counter GT down play, the quarterback should fake the 22 trap play to the fullback, give the ball to the wing, and then fake the counter boot.

• X left 25 counter GT down vs. the 43 defense (Diagram 13-34)

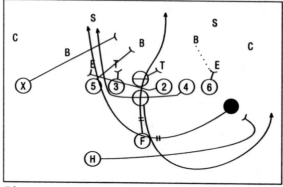

Diagram 13-34

• X left 25 counter GT vs. the 44 defense (Diagram 13-35)

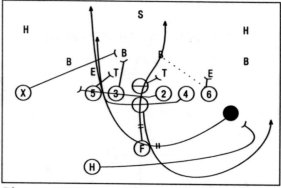

Diagram 13-35

• X left 25 counter GT down vs. the eagle defense (Diagram 13-36)

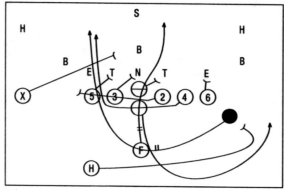

Diagram 13-36

About the Author

Carl O. "Bill" Gentry was born in Slaton, Texas in 1926. Following graduation from Slaton High School, he served in the United States Navy during World War II. After his service in the Navy, Bill attended Coffeyville Junior College in Coffeyville, Kansas for two years. He then attended the University of New Mexico in Albuquerque, from which he graduated with B.S. and M.S. degrees.

In 1958, Bill became the head football coach at Highland High School in Albuquerque, New Mexico. After 31 years at Highland, Bill left Highland to become the head football coach at Eldorado High School in Albuquerque, before the 1989 season. Bill spent seven years at Eldorado, before retiring after the 1995 season. In almost four decades as a head coach, Bill's overall record was 305-102-5. His teams averaged winning eight games per year for 38 years. His teams appeared in the state finals 10 times, winning the New Mexico state championship three times.

In recognition of his extraordinary accomplishments, Coach Gentry was named National High School Football Coach of the Year in 1994 by the National High School Athletic Coaches Association. He has also been inducted into the National High School Hall of Fame, the Albuquerque Sports Hall of Fame, the New Mexico High School Athletic Coaches Association Hall of Honor, and the University of New Mexico Lobo Hall of Honor.

Currently, Bill lives in Albuquerque, New Mexico, with his wife of more than five decades, Mary. In his leisure time, Bill likes walking, camping, trout fishing, and bird hunting.